Folens History Boo[k]

Invasion, plague and murder
Britain 1066 – 1485

Aaron Wilkes

Editorial Consultant: Phil Smith

United Kingdom: Folens Publishers, Apex Business Centre, Boscombe Road, Dunstable, LU5 4RL.

Email: folens@folens.com

Ireland: Folens Publishers, Greenhills Road, Tallaght, Dublin 24.

Email: info@folens.ie

Poland: JUKA, ul. Renesansowa 38, Warsaw 01-905.

Editor: Melanie Gray

Layout artist: Neil Sutton, Pumpkin House Cambridge

Cover design: Martin Cross

First published 2003 by Folens Limited.
Reprinted 2004.

British Library Cataloguing in Publication Data. A catalogue record for this publication is available from the British Library.

ISBN 1 84303 405 0

Acknowledgements

Ashmolean Museum, Oxford: 8 (right); Bibliotheque Nationale, Paris, France/Bridgeman Art Library: 96 (both); Bodleian Library, Oxford: 88 (bottom); Bridgeman Art Library: 6, 48, 73; Bridgeman Art Library/ Lauros / Giraudon: 7; British Library, Shelfmark: Cott.Jul.E.IV art.6 f.20v, Shelfmark/Man: Cott.Tib.C.II.F5v: 9 (bottom), Shelfmark/Man: Cott.Faust.B. F72v: 33, Shelfmark/Man: Sloane.1977.F2: 70, Shelfmark/Man: Roy.18.E.I.F175 Det: 75, Shelfmark/Man:Harl.4751.F23: 89 (top), Shelfmark/Man: Add.42130.F172v Det: 89 (bottom), Shelfmark/Man: Add.42130.F 147v.Det: 103; CADW: Welsh Historic Monuments, Crown Copyright: 58; English Heritage Photographic Library: 40, 49; Fortean Picture Library: 88 (top); Michael Holford: 8 (left), 9 (top), 20, 36, 39; Kobal Collection/ Icon/ Ladd Co/ Paramount: 59; Mary Evans Picture Library: 86; Master & Fellows of Trinity College Cambridge, MS0.1.20,f242v: 67; National Portrait Gallery: 99 (both); Royal Collection Enterprises Limited: 57; Sporting Pictures (UK) Ltd: 87; Wellcome trust Medical Photographic Library: 63

Cover image: Battle of Crecy, 26 August 1346.
Chronique d'Angleterre, (15th Century).
Bibliotheque Nationale, Paris, France/Bridgeman Art Library.

Contents

What is history?

Before you start this book, take a few minutes to think about these questions.

- What do you think history is? What does the word mean?
- What have you learnt in history lessons before, perhaps in your primary school? Did you enjoy them or not? If you enjoyed them, say why. If you didn't enjoy them, why not?
- Have you read any history books or stories about things that happened a long time ago? Have you watched any television programmes, films or plays about things that happened in the past? If so, which ones?

History is about what happened in the past. It is about people in the past, what they did and why they did it, what they thought and what they felt. To enjoy history you need to have a good imagination. You need to be able to imagine what life was like in the past, or what it may have been like to be involved in past events.

How did people feel, think and react to events like these?

History lessons don't just get you to use your imagination; they fill your minds with amazing answers to fascinating questions.

- Which king died after his bladder burst open?
- Whose brains were kicked around a church floor?
- Why was football banned in 1331?
- What disgusting job did a gong farmer do?

History shows us how, why and when things have changed. At one time the king ruled all on his own. He could do what he wanted. He might ask his supporters, barons or earls for some help now and again, but ordinary people had no power at all. The king made the laws and everyone had to do what he said.

A few people were very rich, but most were very poor. The poor lived a hard life – if they got sick, they usually died. If they didn't work hard on their land, they usually starved. Few people cared.

Times have changed a lot since the Middle Ages. Today we have parliament, elections, law courts, hospitals and education for all. We have a queen, but she has very little real power compared with kings and queens of the Middle Ages.

If we want to understand the world around us today, it's important that we know how it came to be this way.

How to use this book

- Most topics in this book include WISE UP WORDS like the ones below.

These are special words that will help you to understand the section properly. You can spot them easily because they are in **bold** type. Look them up in a dictionary or use the glossary at the end of this book. The glossary is a list of words and their meanings.

- Some topics contain PAUSE FOR THOUGHT boxes. This is an opportunity for you to stop and think for yourself. Talk through your views with a classmate or during class discussion.

- The HUNGRY FOR MORE? features give you a chance to extend your knowledge and research beyond the classroom. This is a time for you to take responsibility for your own learning. You might be asked to research something in the library or on the internet, work on a presentation, or design and make something. Can you meet the challenge?

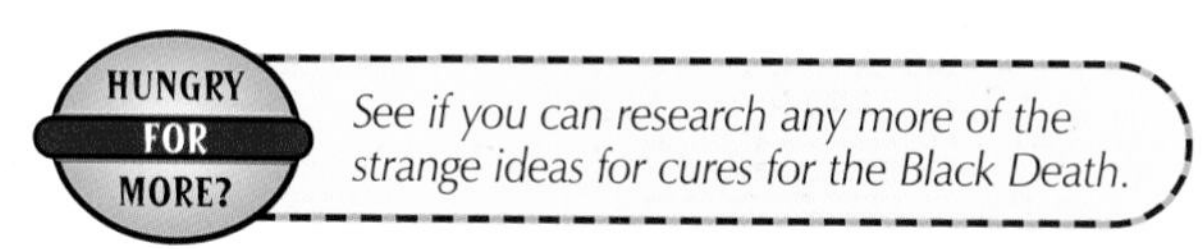

This book will ask you to think. You will be asked to look at pieces of evidence to try to work things out for yourself. Sometimes two pieces of evidence about the same event won't agree with each other. You might be asked to think of reasons why. Your answers might not be the same as your friends' or even your teacher's answers. The important thing is to give reasons for your thoughts and answers.

Good luck!

England before 1066: What was it like?

Imagine this:

- A foreign army invades England.
- The invaders kill the **monarch** and replace him with their own king.
- Nearly all English people with important jobs are replaced by the invaders.
- The new rulers punish anyone who tries to stop the changes by either killing them or starving them to death.
- Old English buildings are pulled down and replaced by ones built by the invaders.
- A new language is introduced.

Surely this could never happen? It did, in 1066, when a foreign army invaded England. All of the things listed above didn't happen straight away. They happened over a number of years, but, even so, after 1066 England was never the same again.

To understand how amazing the changes were, we first need to look at what England was like before the invading army came.

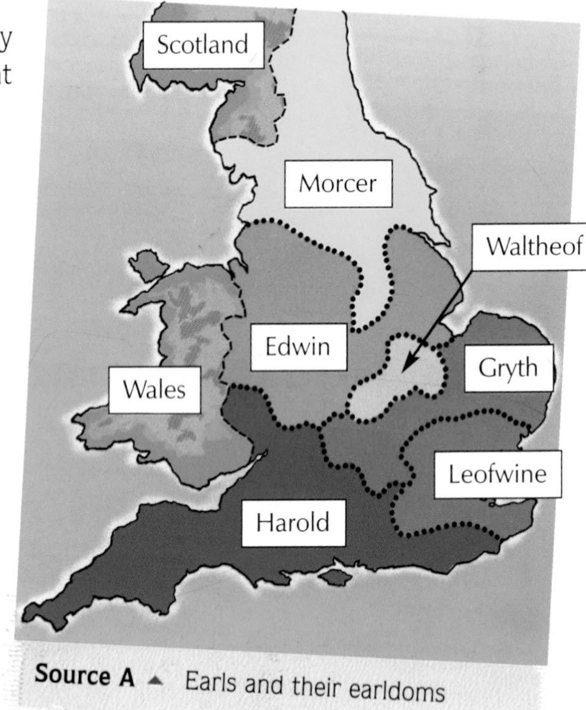

Source A ▲ Earls and their earldoms

Who ruled England before 1066?

The Romans ruled England up to about 470. Then tribes from Germany called Angles and Saxons invaded and stayed here.

PAUSE FOR THOUGHT

How do you think England got its name?

Source B ▲ Edward the Confessor, king of England from 1042 to 1066

From the year 800 onwards, **Vikings** from Denmark and Sweden invaded and also stayed here. The Vikings lived mainly in the north and east of England, while the **Anglo-Saxons** lived in the west and the south. The two sides fought each other for many years but had started to live well alongside each other by 1065.

Edward the Confessor ruled England in 1065. He didn't have to take advice from anyone. Being king was a tough job, so he was helped by six men from rich, important families. They each looked after an area of England called an **earldom**. These men were known as **earls**.

How many people lived in England in 1066?

The population of the whole of England was about 1.5 million people. Nearly everyone worked on the land as farmers. They lived in small villages and probably spent most of their lives there. There were only about seven towns with more than 2500 people living in them - London (the largest), York, Norwich, Stamford, Thetford, Wallingford and Winchester.

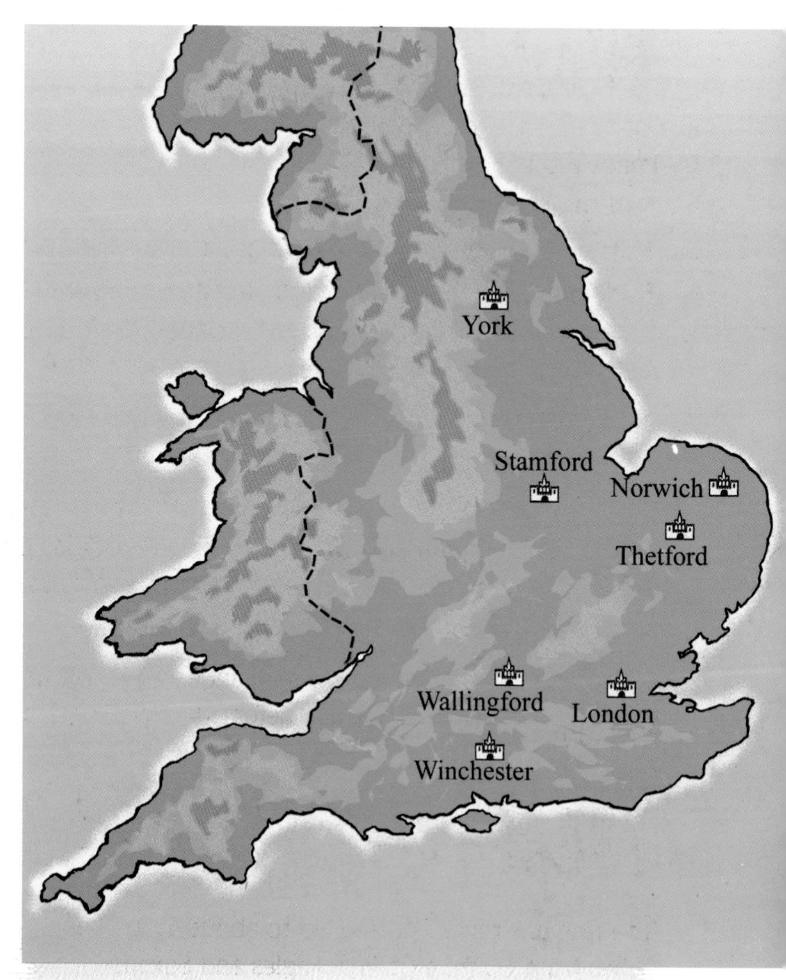

Source c ▲ The seven largest towns in 1066

Source D ▲ England's farmers were some of the best in Europe. An image from a medieval book.

PAUSE FOR THOUGHT

Why do you think we don't know exactly how many people lived in England in 1066?

WISE UP WORDS

chronicles earldom earls evidence monarch vikings anglo-saxons christian church monks

HUNGRY FOR MORE?

What is England's population today? Are the seven largest cities in England today the same seven as in 1066?

Was England a rich country?

The rich were very rich and the poor were very poor. Out of every 100 people, about two were rich. Some men made their fortunes by selling wool to other countries. They built fine buildings and had the best lifestyle they could afford.

By contrast, life was very hard for the poor. People died of even small wounds and infections. If the harvest was bad, people could easily die of starvation.

Source E ▲ The Alfred Jewel, which was made of gold and precious stones. Around the edge it reads 'Alfred had me made.' Alfred was an Anglo-Saxon king from 871 to 901.

Source F ◄ Anglo-Saxon coins. The money system used in 1065 was still being used in England up to 1974.

Were people religious?

The simple answer is 'yes'. Everyone was a Christian and went to church. In monasteries (large churches), monks kept large official diaries called chronicles. They wrote about religion, politics, history, towns, kings, gossip and the weather.

Source G ◂ The Anglo-Saxon church of St Lawrence at Bradford on Avon, Wiltshire

Source H ▸ A page from a monk's chronicle

How do we know all this?

We don't know everything about England in 1066. However, we know enough to give us a good idea about what life was like. We can look at a number of things from Anglo-Saxon times which allow us to build up a idea of life in 1066 – pictures, paintings, churches, jewellery and books. These things are called **evidence**.

WORK

1 Many of the sources used in this book were written by chroniclers. These were men who wrote chronicles. They often had their own point of view and wrote about what they believed and felt, rather than what they actually saw. Why is it important to know this when studying history?

2 Use pages 6-9 to write your own fact file about England in 1066. You should use ten sentences to write ten different facts. Add the title "My top ten facts about England in 1066."

3 The beginnings and endings of these sentences have been mixed up. Using the information on these two pages, match up the start of the sentences (List A) with the correct ending (List B).

List A	List B
Romans, Anglo-Saxons and Vikings	was about 1.5 million
London	were some of the best in Europe
England's farmers	have all invaded England at one time or another
Edward the Confessor	was England's largest town in 1066
The population of England in 1066	was King of England in 1066

Who will be king of England?

- Why was there a struggle for the English throne in 1066?
- Who were the three main contenders for the throne?

1066 is one of the most famous dates in history, and many of you will have heard the date before. 1066 was the last time that England was successfully invaded by a foreign power. Invading foreigners killed the English king and his supporters and divided up the country between themselves. The new rulers introduced a new language. They ruled over the country with strict control and changed the course of British history.

The old king dies

In January 1066, Edward the Confessor, king of England, died. He was 62 years old. With no children there was no **heir** to the throne. Three men believed that they should be the next king, and they were prepared to kill to get the crown.

The Englishman

Name:	Harold Godwinson
Position:	Earl of Wessex, one of the most powerful men in England.
Family history:	His father, Godwin, argued a lot with King Edward. At one time Harold and his father were banished from England, but they returned a year later.
Links to King Edward:	Harold's sister was married to King Edward.
Was he tough enough?	Harold was a brave and respected soldier with a tough streak. In 1063 King Edward sent Harold to crush a Welsh **uprising**. The Welsh leader was caught and his head was chopped off on Harold's orders.
Support for his claim:	He was the only Englishman claiming the throne. The **Witan**, a meeting of the most important bishops and earls in England, wanted Harold to be the next king. English monks wrote: 'Harold and his brothers were the king's favourites... on his deathbed that wise king promised the kingdom to Harold.'

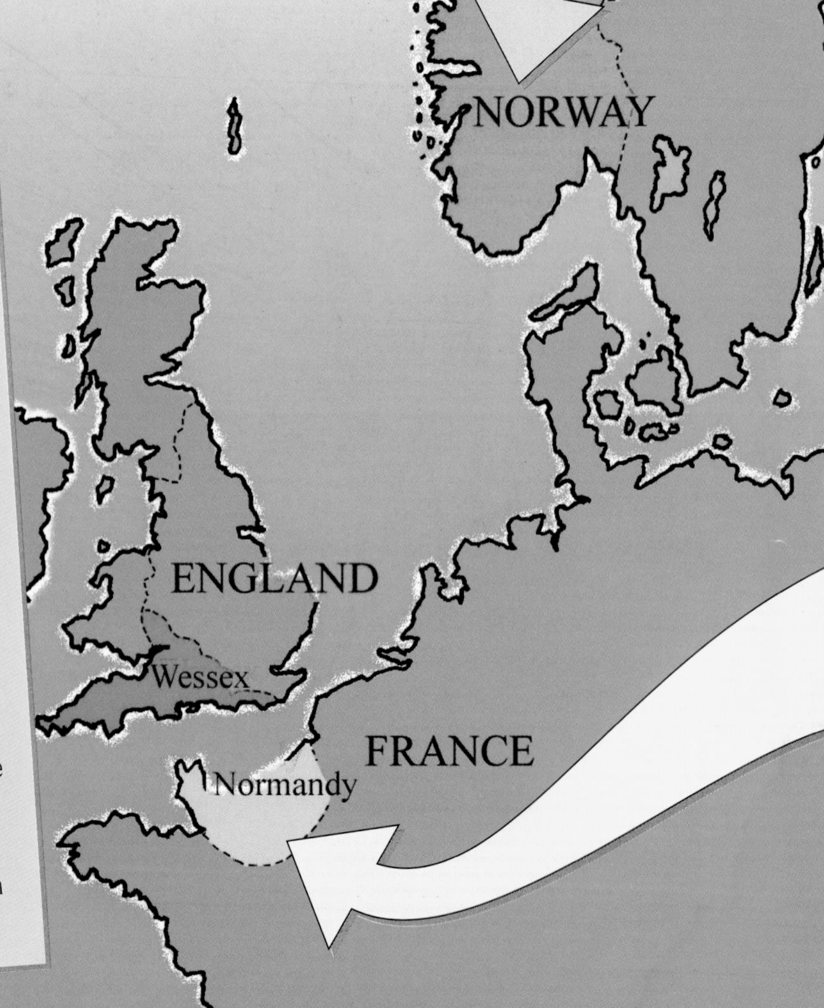

The Viking

Name: Harald Hardrada

Position: King of Norway

Family history: He had fought alongside several Norwegian kings and had taken part in raids on the English coast. When he became king of Norway, he began to plan a full-scale invasion of England.

Links to King Edward: None – but a Viking called Canute had ruled Norway and England from 1016 to 1035.

Was he tough enough? He was the most feared warrior in Europe – tough, bloodthirsty and he enjoyed watching his enemies suffer. Hardrada means 'hard ruler' and his nickname was 'The Ruthless'.

Support for his claim: Harald's claim was supported by Tostig, Harold Godwinson's brother. The two brothers had fallen out and Tostig wanted revenge.

The Norman

Name: William of Normandy

Position: Duke of Normandy, the strongest part of France.

Family history: William came from a fighting family. He had been in control of Normandy since he was seven and was used to having to fight to keep his lands.

Links to King Edward: Edward had lived in Normandy from 1016 to 1042. When Edward returned to England to be king, William sent soldiers to help him. As a result King Edward had promised William the throne in 1051.

Was he tough enough? His nickname was William the Bastard because his father wasn't married to his mother. In 1047 people from the town of Alençon made fun of his mother's family. William captured the town and ordered that 30 of the townsmen be skinned alive.

Support for his claim: According to William of Poitiers, a **Norman** writer, 'Edward, king of the English, loved William like a brother or son...' so he decided that William should be the next king.' Harold Godwinson had visited William to tell him this news in 1064 and promised to support William's claim to the English crown.

- **Harold Godwinson's men**: Harold was English and his followers were Englishmen. At this time, England is sometimes known as Saxon England so the people are sometimes called Saxons.
- **Harald Hardrada's men**: Hardrada and his men were from Norway. Invaders from this country were known as Vikings.
- **William of Normandy's men**: William and his followers come from a region in France called Normandy. People from there are known as Normans.

When King Edward died on 5 January 1066, Harold had one great advantage over his two rivals. William and Hardrada were miles away across the sea in different countries. Harold was in England and was crowned the very next day. However, Harold knew that news would soon reach the other two that England had a new king. Harold knew they would come looking for him, and that they'd both want him dead.

A bad omen?

In April 1066 a comet was visible in the sky over England. The people could see it for a week. They thought this meant that terrible times lay ahead.

WORK

Now you have read about the three contenders for the throne, you must decide who you think had the best claim (reason to be king).

1 Copy and complete the following table. Try to include as many reasons as possible.

Contender	Why they should be king	Why they shouldn't be king
Harold Godwinson		
Harald Hardrada		
William of Normandy		

2 List the three contenders in the order that you think had the strongest claim. Label your first choice 'strongest' and your last choice 'weakest'.

3 In your own words, explain why you placed the three contenders in the order you have chosen.

Round one: The Battle of Stamford Bridge

- How did Harold end Hardrada's claim to the throne?
- What were the consequences of the battle for Harold and William?

In early September 1066, King Harold of England received some devastating news. Hardrada, king of Norway, had landed near York. Tostig, Harold's younger brother, was with him and so were about 10,000 bloodthirsty Viking soldiers.

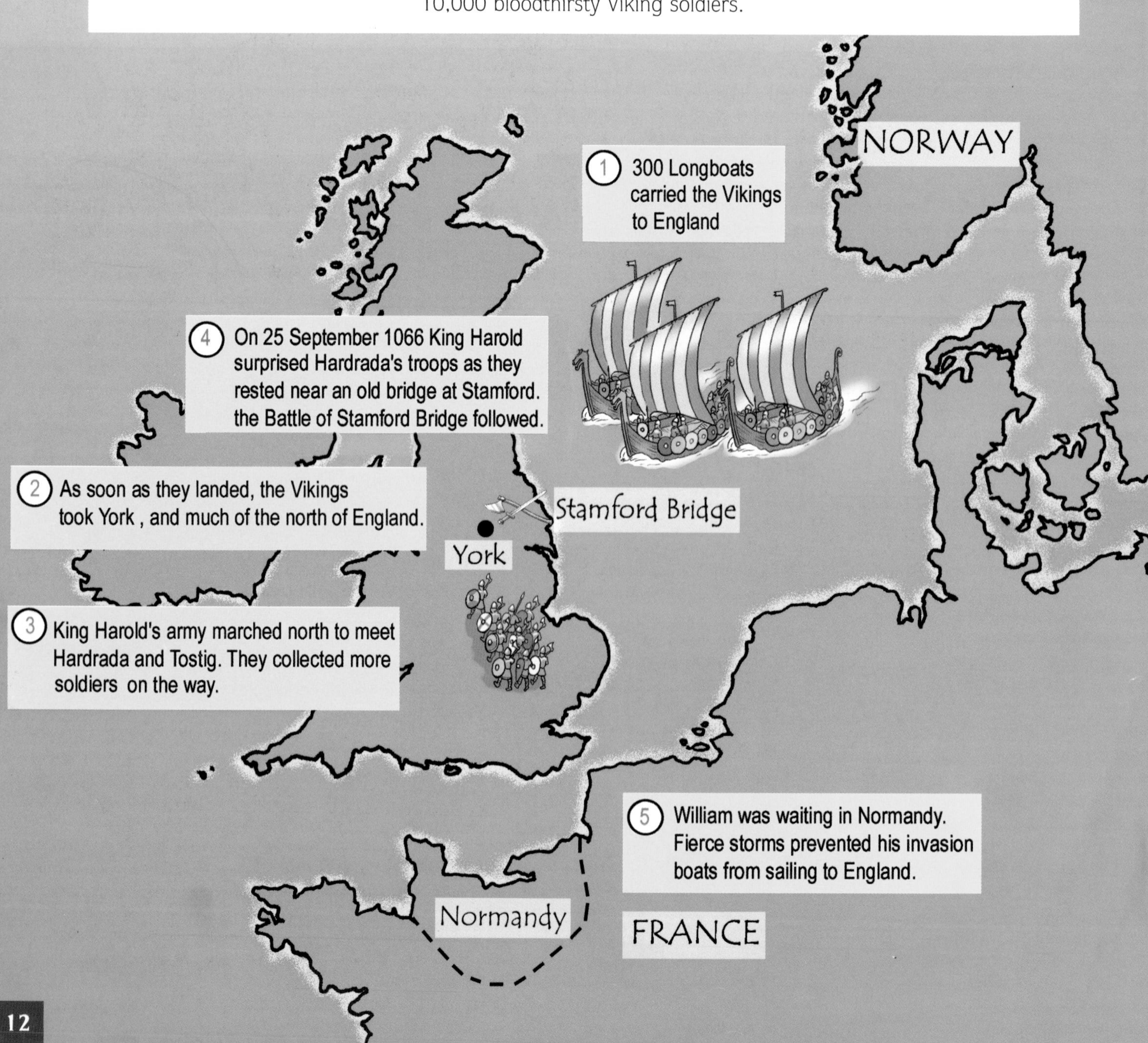

WORK

1 The following statements are all reasons explaining why King Harold defeated Hardrada at the Battle of Stamford Bridge. Write down these statements in the correct **chronological order**.
- The Viking warrior blocking the bridge was killed.
- The few Vikings still alive escaped in four ships.
- Hardrada was killed.
- The Vikings didn't expect to see Harold's army so soon.
- Many of Hardrada's men did not have their armour.

2 What do you believe was the key turning point in helping Harold win the Battle of Stamford Bridge? Give reasons for your answer.

3 Many Viking warriors ran away when Hardrada was killed. Can you explain why they might have done this?

Match of the day!

- What were the events leading to the Battle of Hastings?
- What arms and weapons were used by Harold's and William's forces?

Harold's housecarls
(current champions)
v
William's knights
(the challengers)

Date: 14 October 1066
Venue: Senlac Hill, near Hastings
Kick-off: 9.30am

King Harold has some superb soldiers, in particular the fearsome **housecarls** – well paid, fully trained and armed with the finest weapons money can buy. There are about 2,500 of these long-haired, bearded warriors. Let's have a look at them.

Source A ▸ An English housecarl and members of the fyrd

As well as the housecarls, King Harold is also supported by about 2000 of the **fyrd**. This mobile army isn't as experienced as the housecarls but it's still a fierce fighting force. Local **peasants** armed with scythes, pitchforks and axes will also help their king.

In total there are about 8000 English soldiers. Duke William has a long, hard battle on his hands if he wants to defeat them.

FACT: Weapons file

- **Axe** This is the main English weapon. It can cut down a man or a horse with little effort. The blade is made of iron – a very precious metal in 1066 – with a heat-welded steel edge. The handle is at least a metre long.

The Normans have been waiting for this day ever since Harold was crowned in January. Duke William's invasion force is massive: over 300 ships, 10,000 men and 2000 horses. He's even brought along his own wooden fort. They landed at Pevensey on 28 September and soon moved on to Hastings, deciding to set fire to the town to annoy King Harold even more. The Normans have archers and crossbowmen, foot soldiers and **cavalry** (men on horses). It all looks very impressive.

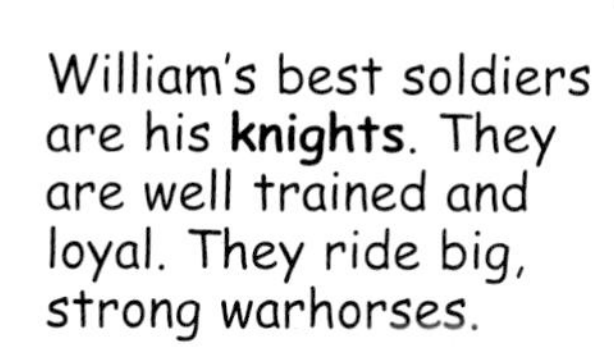

William's best soldiers are his **knights**. They are well trained and loyal. They ride big, strong warhorses.

FACT: Weapons file

- **Sword** A very heavy and very sharp weapon, about a metre in length.

- **Bows and arrows** The archers are equipped with small wooden bows and are able to fire six or seven arrows a minute. A well-aimed arrow could kill a man or a horse from about 180 metres away.
- **Crossbow** These shoot a bolt, released by a trigger, over 100 metres. They take longer to load than a bow but are feared by all who face them.

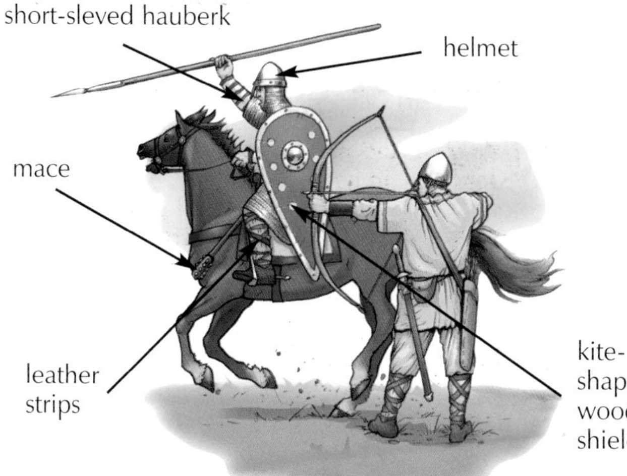

Source B ▲ A Norman knight on horseback and an archer

WORK

1 Match up the words on the left with the correct description on the right.

Housecarl	Can fire six or seven arrows per minute.
Fyrd	Mobile army of about 2000 Englishmen.
Peasants	Harold's best soldiers. Armed with double-handed axes.
Archers	Well trained and fully armed. They ride strong warhorses.
Foot soldiers	Poorly armed, poorly trained local Englishmen.
Knights	Fought on foot. An important part of William's army.

2 Which side was best prepared for battle? Give reasons for your answer.

Round two: The Battle of Hastings - the morning

AIMS
- What were the battle tactics of Harold and William?
- What was the outcome of the early stages of the battle?

King Harold could hardly believe his bad luck. His battered and bruised army had just defeated Hardrada, Tostig and the Viking army at Stamford Bridge and now they were going to have to fight all over again. They had to march hundreds of miles south to meet the new invaders. On the night of 11 October, after nearly two weeks of marching, King Harold and his army set up camp on a hill about 10 kilometres away from William's army at Hastings. The hill became known as Senlac Hill – the Norman translation means 'lake of blood'.

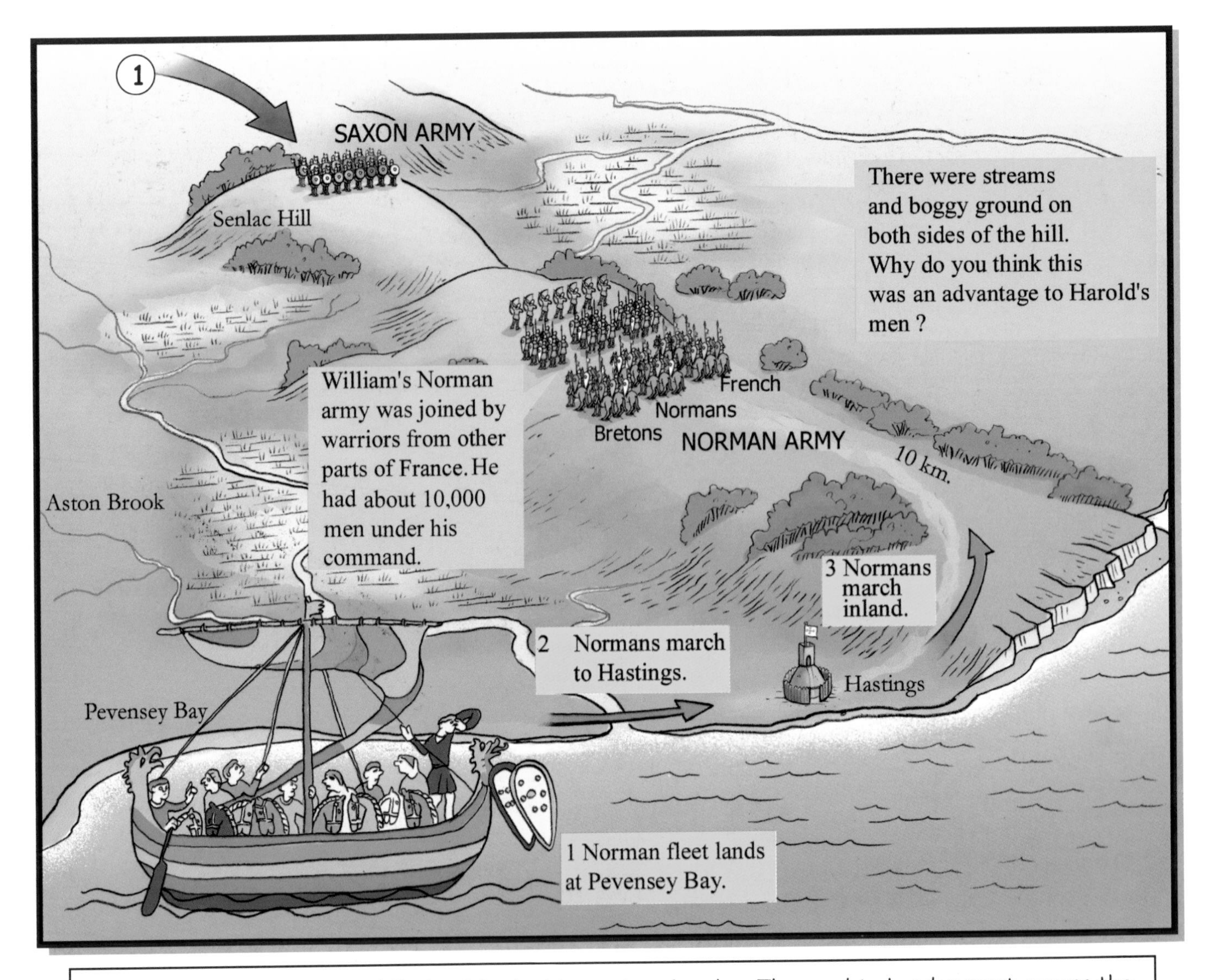

If William wanted to control England, he had to capture London. The road to London went across the top of Senlac Hill. To get to London, William had to defeat Harold's army.

The battle started at about 9.30am as the Normans fired arrows and then the knights charged up the hill on their horses. The foot soldiers had to climb up the steep hill as well and they must have been exhausted by the time they started fighting.

William told his men that they weren't just fighting for victory, they were fighting for their lives.

◂ William believed he had God on his side, so he carried the sign of the Christian cross on a flag given to him by the Pope.

▸ Harold's army beat the back of their shields with their swords. They shouted "out! out! out!" at the Normans

Some men asked King Harold to let his brothers Gyrth and Leofwine do the fighting for him. Harold refused and said: 'William the Bastard shall never hear that I dare not look him in the face.'

The battle raged for over two hours. During this time the English stood firm behind their **shield wall**. Then a rumour started to spread among the soldiers – nobody had seen William for half an hour.

▸ "Look at me! Look at me! I'm alive, and with God's help, will be the victor."

William wasn't dead at all. He had galloped forward to face his men and lifted his helmet so everyone could see his determined face. What effect do you think this had on his army?

WORK

1 Separate the following list into factors that would help Harold win the battle and factors that would help William win the battle. Use a large copy of the table (right) to help you.

- Harold's men had just come from a fierce battle with Hardrada.
- Harold put his men at the top of Senlac Hill.
- There were streams and boggy ground on both sides of Senlac Hill.
- William had a large army of about 10,000 men.
- The road to London went over Senlac Hill.
- William's army had been blessed by the **Pope**.
- The housecarls protected Harold's army with a strong shield wall.

Factors that would help help Harold win the battle	Factors that would help William win the battle

2 Overall, which side do you think was best prepared for the Battle of Hastings?

3 Which side do you think performed the best during the morning's fighting? Try to give some reasons for your answer.

Round two: The Battle of Hastings – the afternoon

AIMS
- How did William win at Hastings?
- What were William's first moves after defeating Harold?

After a brief break in the fighting, the battle started again at around 12.30pm. Neither side seemed to be winning. The Normans kept attacking but the English were holding them off behind their strong shield wall. At about 3.30pm, William had an idea. Read boxes 1 and 2 to see what the idea was.

The idea was a stroke of genius. Normans on horses pretended to run away. Englishmen on foot followed them down the hill and out into the open.

On their horses, William's men easily caught up with the Englishmen and cut them to pieces.

William hoped the English would fall for the trick again – which they did. The Norman knights pretended to run away several times. Gradually the English shield wall on top of Senlac Hill became weaker as King Harold's men ran down the hill after the Normans on horses.

According to some sources, William fought bravely during the battle (see **Sources C + D**).

Source C Taken from a history textbook.

Three horses were killed under him. Three times he leapt unafraid to the ground and killed the man who had killed his horse. This shows how quick he was to make his mind up and how strong he was.

With savage blows of his sword, he split shields, helmets and coats of chain mail. He struck a number of enemies with his own shield. His soldiers took new courage when they saw him fighting on foot. Some, who were weak from bleeding, leant on their shields and fought on bravely. William himself helped some of his men to safety.

He led his forces with great skill, holding them when they turned to run, giving them courage, sharing their danger. He was more often heard shouting to them to follow him than ordering them to go on ahead. It is clear that it was the Duke's bravery that inspired his soldiers as they went forward and gave them courage.

Source D ▸ An account of William fighting in the battle, written in 1073

▸ William then turned to his archers, who started to rain arrows down on Harold and his men.

Why was this such a good idea?

▸ At about 6pm Harold was killed. He may have been wounded by an arrow in his eye first.

As King Harold falls to the floor, four Norman knights break through the weakening shield wall and cut him to pieces.

As well as a feast, the Normans robbed the dead bodies. They took all their chain mail, leather shoes, swords, axes and helmets – why do you think they did this?

WISE UP WORDS

cavalry chronological order disembowelled dysentery fyrd heir housecarl knights norman peasants pope shield wall symptoms uprising witan

Summary

- Harold became King of England in January 1066. Two other men wanted the crown – Hardrada of Norway and William of Normandy.
- Harold defeated Hardrada at Stamford Bridge, but was killed at the Battle of Hastings by William's forces. William became King in December 1066.

What happened next?

Harold's body was identified that evening. He had been **disembowelled**, so the body must have been a horrific sight. William ordered that the body be taken away and buried near the seashore.

On the night of 14 October 1066, William only ruled as far as he could see. Early the next morning William and his army left Senlac Hill and marched towards London. He made sure that all the towns he found along the way surrendered to him. More and more soldiers from Normandy flooded into England. By early December, William had reached London and he was crowned King on Christmas Day.

An enemy within!

William was not defeated in battle, but he was nearly defeated by **dysentery**. On the way to London, William's army was struck by an outbreak of dysentery. The **symptoms** were stomach ache and terrible diarrhoea. Some soldiers had to return to France and others died. However, some remained fit enough to continue on to London.

WORK

1 Read **Source C + D**.
   a Write down five words to describe William during the Battle of Hastings.
   b Do you think the writer of Source D was Norman or English? Why?
   c Is this source a reliable piece of evidence? What do you need to know about it to say how reliable it is?

2 You should now know about what happened at the Battle of Hastings. It's time to make up your mind – why did William win the battle? Was it:
   - because he was a brilliant and skilful leader?
   - because Harold was a poor soldier who made mistakes?
   - because the Normans were better equipped and prepared?
   - because Harold was unlucky?

   Or was it a combination of all or some of these reasons?

HISTORY MYSTERY

How did King Harold die?

Historians (people who study history – like you!) are like detectives who hunt for clues and piece them together. If they find enough evidence, a clear picture emerges.

The death of King Harold is one of the biggest mysteries of the Battle of Hastings. We know he died – he must have done because a new king began ruling England – but we don't know exactly how he died.

Historians know a great deal about the events of 1066 and the Battle of Hastings. Some people wrote about it at the time; others told stories about it, which were then written down; and some people made pictures showing it. The problem with King Harold's death is that the sources (pieces of evidence) don't always agree about what happened.

Your job as a history mystery detective is to look through the evidence and decide what you think. By the end of this topic you must answer the question: How did King Harold die?

Evidence A

Date: 1068
Writer: A Norman monk, name unknown

With the point of his **lance** the first knight pierced Harold's shield and chest, drenching the ground with blood. With his sword the second knight cut off his head. The third knight disembowelled him with his javelin. The fourth hacked off his leg.

Evidence B

Date: 1070–71
Writer: William of Jumieges, a Norman monk. He claims he was at the battle. His **abbey** was given money by William the Conqueror.

Duke William engaged the enemy at the third hour [about 9am] and continued until nightfall. Harold fell in the first shock of the battle, pierced with lethal wounds.

Evidence C

Date: About 1077
Writers: The women of Bayeux, Normandy.

The women made a tapestry on the orders of Bishop Odo, William's brother. Odo was at the battle. The Bayeux Tapestry is about 70m long and half a metre wide, with over 70 panels. "Harold Rex interfectus est" means "here King Harold dies."

Evidence D

Date: 1125

Writer: William of Malmesbury, a monk. Historians believe this source was written after he had seen the Bayeux Tapestry.

Harold continued; but when he fell, from having his brain pierced with an arrow... he yielded to death... one of the soldiers with a sword gashed his thigh as he lay.

Evidence E

Date: 2000

Writer: Simon Schama, a modern historian who presents history programmes for the BBC.

How did Harold himself die? Lately there's been an attempt to read the death scene in the Bayeux Tapestry as though he was the figure cut down by the horsemen, not the warrior pulling the arrow out of his eye... but it seems to me perfectly clear that the words 'Harold Rex' occur directly and significantly above the arrow-struck figure... then certainly the knights would have been on him.

FACT: How do opinions differ?

- There are some things that we just don't know about the past. Some historians say the evidence proves how Harold was killed. Others say it proves we can't be sure. These disagreements are one of the things that make history so fascinating.

WORK

To try to solve this mystery, you need to look closely at all the evidence.

1. **Find out all the different ways Harold may have died.**

   What weapons were used? At what stage of the battle did he die? Make a list of your findings.

2. **Find out if any of the evidence agrees on how Harold was killed.**

   Does any one piece of evidence back up what another says? Write down notes on what you have found.

3. **Think - can you trust the evidence?**

   Write down why you might not trust some of the evidence. You may believe all the evidence is useful or perhaps just some of it. Do we have an English eyewitness to Harold's death? If not, why not?

4. **Now make your decision.**

   Like a detective, use evidence to back up your theory. If you're not sure, say why. In history it's OK to say you're uncertain, as long as you can explain why.

How did William control England?

- What were William's methods for controlling his new kingdom?
- How important were motte and bailey castles?

William was crowned in London on Christmas Day 1066. The new king of England was a Frenchman, who spoke French and had French friends. Most Englishmen hated him... and wanted him dead!

William's solution to controlling his kingdom was simple – terrify people! He wanted to make the English so afraid of him that they wouldn't rebel any more.

Whenever William believed that the English were plotting against him, he sent out his soldiers to crush the plot viciously. William soon got a reputation as a cruel king, and he became known as William the Conqueror.

Respect for the king

In 1069 an English uprising killed all the Normans in Durham. In return, William sent his soldiers to kill all English males around Durham. They burned down houses and set fire to food stores. They killed all the cattle. The new king wanted to teach the English a lesson – anyone who rebelled against him would die. Survivors had to eat what they could – even dead people – or face starvation.

William had brought his rich and powerful friends from France to help him control the English. In return for this support he gave them large areas of English land. These friends became powerful landowners known as **barons**. They soon realised that they needed protection from attacks by unhappy Englishmen. They decided to build castles. By 1086, King William's barons had built over 100 castles all over the country.

Source A ▾ A **motte** and **bailey** castle. Each one took seven to fourteen days to build.

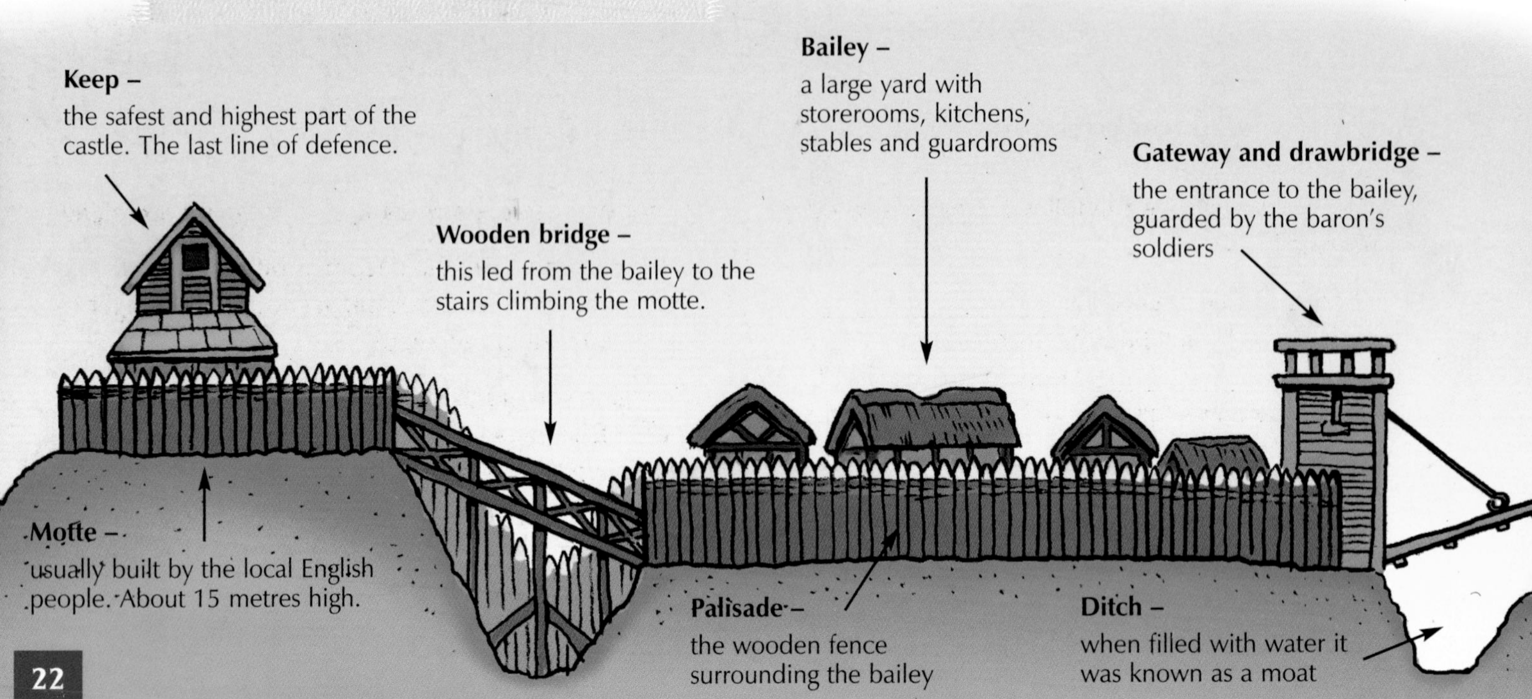

Reduced to rubble

Motte and bailey castles had to be built quickly, and wherever the Normans wanted them. If some houses or a village stood where the baron wanted a castle, he simply built on top of them. In Cambridge 25 houses were pulled down to make way for a new castle. In Lincoln the Normans pulled down over 150 houses. A castle was once built in York in only eight days.

Norman barons and their soldiers used these motte and bailey castles as a base from which they could control the local area. They also became a focus for local trade in the area, which the baron could then tax. However, these wooden castles had one major weakness – fire. It didn't take much for an angry Englishman to shoot a flaming arrow into the bailey or on to the **keep** roof. The Normans needed something that wouldn't burn. They needed to use stone.

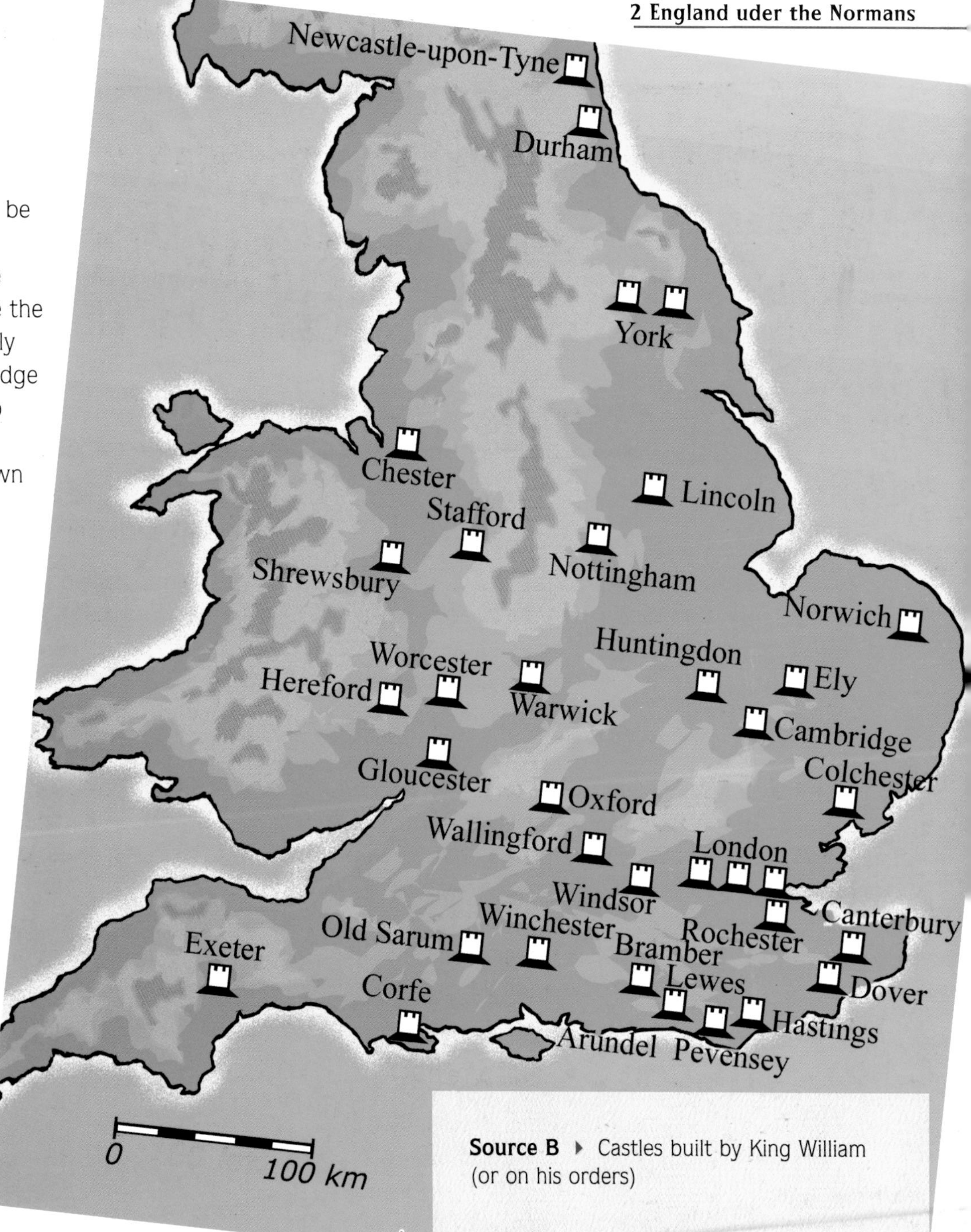

Source B ▸ Castles built by King William (or on his orders)

WORK

1 Copy and complete the following paragraph using the missing words from the list.

Although William was now ____________________ of England, he still had the problem of ____________________ the defeated English. In order to achieve this, one of his favourite tactics was the use of ____________________. Whenever the English caused him trouble, William would send his ____________________ to kill all those involved. Another tactic used by William to control the people of England was the building of ____________________.

terror • soldiers • castles • king • controlling

2 Why do you think the keep was built on a high earth mound? What advantages would the height give to those in the keep?

3 Imagine you are an angry Englishman who has just led a failed attack on a motte and bailey castle. Describe the obstacles you faced on the way to the keep before you were finally defeated. Remember to include what you think were the weaknesses of the wooden castle.

Stone castles: How did they keep the enemy out?

- Why were stone castles built?
- How were stone castles designed and what features did they have?
- What different tactics were used for defending and attacking castles?

Although wooden castles were easy to build and helped William to quickly control the English, they burned easily and they rotted. As a result, William introduced stone as a building material. One of these early stone castles is the Tower of London, which was started in 1078.

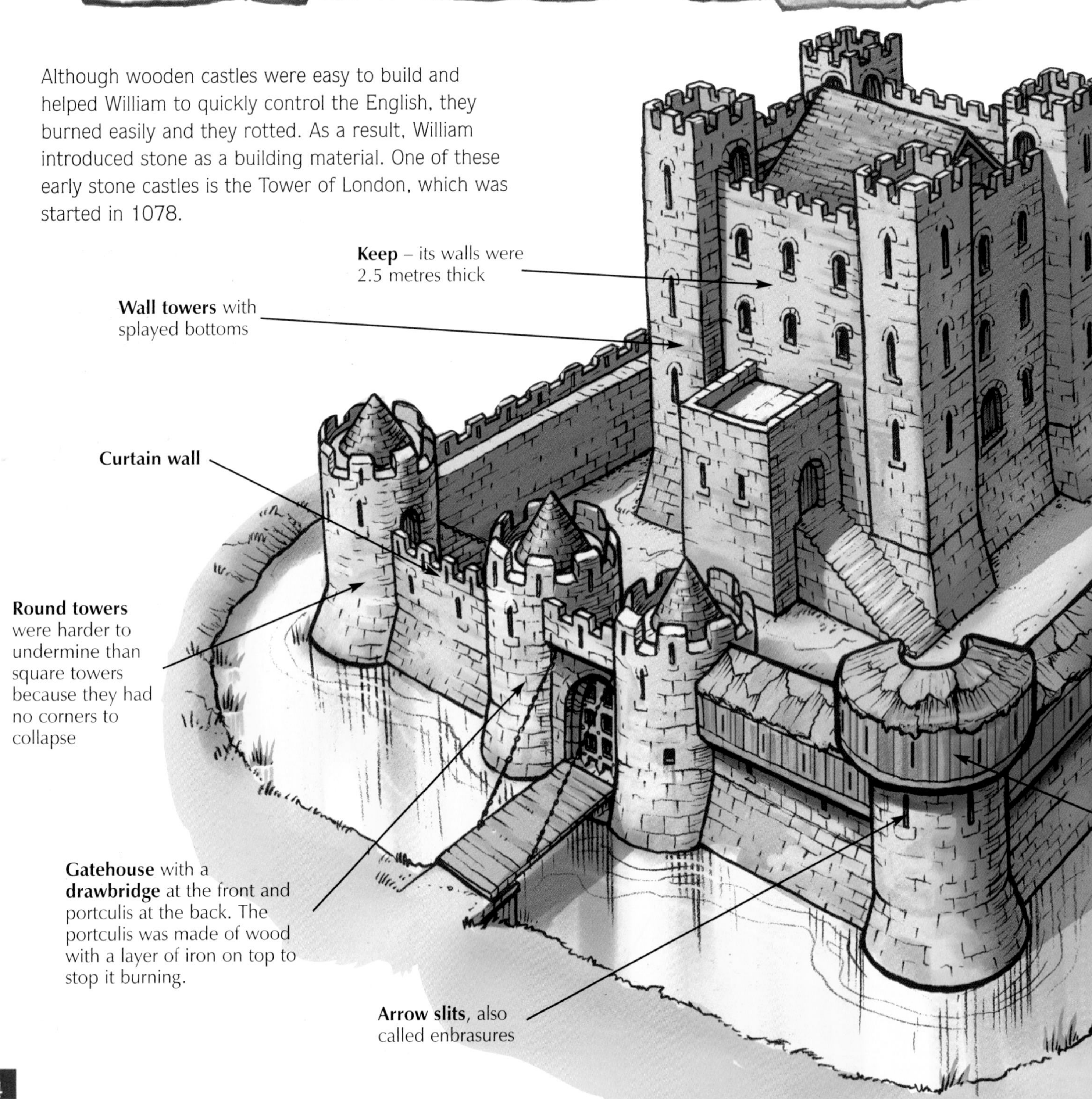

Part of the reason for building a stone castle was to create an impression. The baron wanted to show everyone that he was in charge. The castle was also his safe base from which he could rule the local area. There was no fixed plan or shape to a castle, so each one was different depending on how the baron wanted it constructed. The common factor in all castles was that the baron wanted it to be very difficult to break into. So castle builders used every trick possible to keep the enemy out.

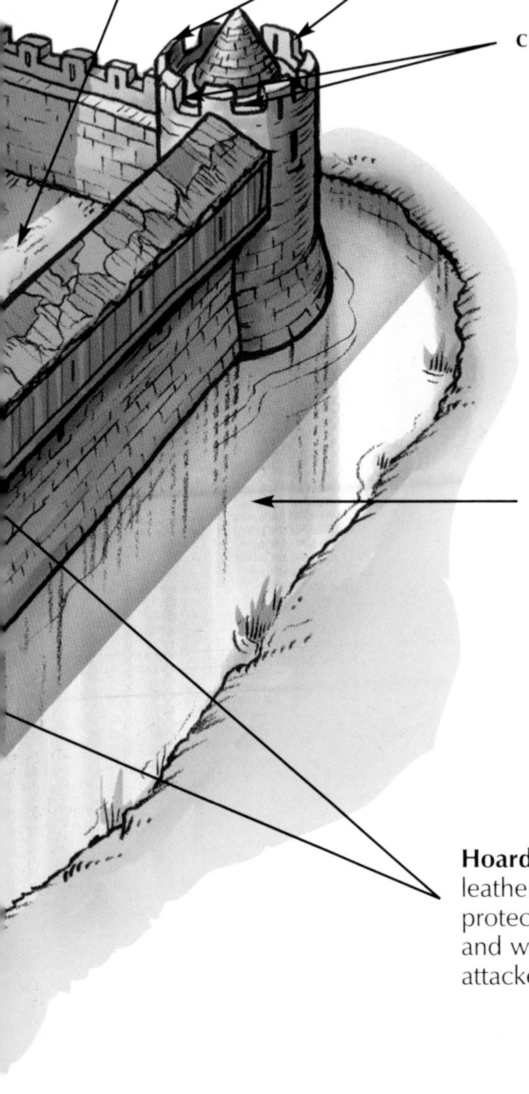

Bailey – a safe place to shelter during attack

Merlons (raised stonework)

crenels (gaps)

Moat – the only safe way across was over the drawbridge

Hoarding with leather cover, used to protect the towers and walls when being attacked

PAUSE FOR THOUGHT

The Baron's aim was to keep the enemy out. He added lots of different features to his castle to achieve this – but did they actually work? As you look through the defences, can you spot anything that might have helped the attackers? For example, the ***crenels*** *were a good place for the enemy to place their ladders to gain entry!*

FACT: Clever gatehouse traps

- Some gatehouses and drawbridges were booby trapped. A trapdoor would drop an unwanted attacker into the drawbridge pit.
- Murder holes were positioned above the main entrance. Defenders could pour boiling water or fire arrows at the enemy from here.
- Arrow slits or peep holes were cleverly disguised inside the gatehouse walls. From inside these passages, soldiers could shoot at unwanted visitors.

WORK

1. Why was a stone castle better than a wooden motte and bailey castle?
2. Give three reasons why a baron would want to spend so much time and money building a stone castle.
3. Imagine you are a wealthy baron about to build a new stone castle. Draw up a short list of requirements to your builder. Make sure you include:
   - information about the different parts of the castle
   - details about the thickness of the walls
   - information about what sort of towers do you want – square or round – and give reasons for your choice
   - details about what the gatehouse will be like – draw a picture to go with your letter
   - a list of different items you would like added to help protect you from your enemies (hoardings, murder holes, etc).

Stone castles: How could the enemy get in?

- What was a siege?
- How did special weapons help an attacking army get into a castle?

Sappers –
specialist soldiers who could fill in a moat with logs, stones or soil. Also they could dig under a wall or tower and collapse it.
The wooden cover they hid under was called a tortoise.

Greek fire –
a mixture of tar, oil and sulphur which could not be put out with water. Only urine could put the fire out!

Battering ram –
a tree trunk hanging on a wooden frame, protected by an animal skin roof.

Siege tower –
a large wooden tower protected by animal skins. In 1216 over 200 soldiers hid in one large tower when attacking Kenilworth Castle.

Trebouchet –
could fire rocks or quicklime. Sometimes rotting animal corpses were even fired into the castle.

Latrine shaft –
the attackers might try and crawl up the shaft, but may get stuck…

Archers –
a skilled archer could fire an arrow over 200 metres, or even straight through the arrow slits in the castle walls.

Mangonel –
another machine used to fire rocks at the castle.

The siege of Rochester Castle

In 1216 a group of **rebel** barons and more than 100 well-armed soldiers took over Rochester Castle. They took action because their king, John, was a poor leader and kept asking them to pay higher taxes. Rochester Castle guarded a main road to London and King John needed control of it. So he decided to **besiege** the castle. This meant that the king and his army surrounded the castle and tried to work out a way of getting in.

The defences of stone castles made them very difficult to break into. One set of walls at Rochester Castle was over four metres thick.

Instead of trying to knock the walls down, starving the men inside until they surrendered was a common way of taking over a castle. However, King John didn't want to waste time doing that. The barons had enough food and water to hold out for weeks, maybe months. To save time, the king instructed his army to use special weapons and tricks to get in and defeat the rebel barons.

When a group of people were defending a castle and another group were attacking, it was called a **siege**.

FACT: Breaking and entering

- In 1166 a young knight and his soldiers were trying to attack Ludlow Castle. He saw a lady at one of the windows and managed to persuade her to let him in. He put his ladder against the wall and climbed through the high window, but he left his ladder there and didn't push it away as he had promised the lady he would. Soon his entire army of soldiers got in through the window and took over the castle. But it didn't all go well for the untrustworthy knight. The lady, so mad that he had broken his promise to her, stabbed him to death in a fit of rage.

Did John enter Rochester castle?

Eventually he did, but it took him several weeks. The **sappers** saved the day. They dug under the castle walls, filled the tunnel with wood and set fire to it. King John even ordered 40 fat pigs to be thrown into the fire. The fat burned so well that one of the castle walls began to crack. Eventually it fell down and the king's army stormed in.

WORK

Now you have read about stone castles it is time to put your knowledge into practice.

The year is 1304 and Stirling Castle is under siege! In pairs you are to imagine the events that took place in the final week of the siege.

1. One person is to take the role of the attacker. Think about what tricks and weapons you could use to get in. The other person is to take the role of the baron, defending his castle. Think about what defences you have for keeping them out.
2. In pairs, discuss the possible events during this last week.
3. Write a siege diary from the point of view of your character. Include all the events of that week. How the siege ends is up to you.

Summary

- Motte and Bailey castles were replaced by stronger stone castles.
- Barons and Knights used castles as bases from which they controlled the surrounding area.
- Stone castles were very difficult to break into, so attackers had to develop many different methods of attack.

The siege of Stirling Castle was a real siege. What can you find out about it? Who was inside and why? Who was trying to get in? Who won?

Who lived in a castle like this?

- What sort of people lived in Norman castles?
- What jobs did they do?
- What was day-to-day castle life like?

I'm the constable and I look after the day-to-day running of this place. I order food, organise repairs and look after the prisoners. All the blacksmiths, carpenters, stonemasons, cooks, tailors and armourers work for me.

Jim Crow's the name and look-out's the game. I spend my days standing high up on the castle walls waiting for people to approach. When I see someone I give a coded blow on my horn.

Don't forget me! I'm the oubliette or 'forgotten prisoner'. I've been pushed into a small, cramped cell and left to die. I haven't been fed and I have no water.

I stink. I'm the gong farmer that's why! My job is to clean out all the garderobes or toilets. In 1326 one of my friends, Richard the Raker, fell through some rotten planks above a garderobe. Locals say 'he drowned monstrously in excrement'.

I am the baron. I own the castle and all the land around it. I even own the peasants working on my land. I spend my money on fantastic food, beautiful wall-hangings from Arras in France, fabulous clothes, gold and silver jewellery and ornaments, and on entertaining my friends.

FACT: Beautiful bed

- One of the baron's most valuable possessions was his bed. Most people slept on the floor with the dirt, bits of food, bones, rats and fleas. Not the baron, however. He slept in luxury in expensive sheets, on top of a straw-filled mattress, held in a beautifully crafted frame.

This man had stolen from the baron. His body is on display as a warning to others. The body will stay here for months. Birds and maggots will eat the flesh until only bones are left.

I'm the castle jester. Sometimes people call me the fool. My job is to tell funny stories and sing rude songs. Even my clothes are silly.

WORK

1. In small groups, act out a day in the life of some of the people in a **medieval** castle. One person is to take on the role of baron making his daily inspection of the castle. As he travels through the building he meets other people who live there. The baron should act out a short scene with each character he meets, while the audience has to guess who he has met and what job they do.
2. Choose one of the characters from the castle. Imagine that they have fallen from the battlements by accident! It's your job to recruit someone to fill their post. Write a job advert to find a replacement. Remember to include a full job description and the skills required for this post.

I've got 14 days to go! As a knight, my main job is to protect the baron and I do this for 40 days a year. I provide all the soldiers too. When my 40 days are over, another knight who lives nearby will come and do his duty.

HUNGRY FOR MORE?

There is probably a medieval castle or some ruins in a town or city near you. Carry out some research and make a presentation on the castle, including:
- *Who built the castle and when?*
- *Did any sieges take place there?*
- *Find out if it has any special features used to protect it from attack.*
- *Try to find out a little bit about who lived in the castle.*
- *Have you visited it? What was it like? How did you find out about its past?*

I bet you're wondering why my pants are a bit sticky. Let me explain. I'm the ale-conner or the beer tester. Everyone drinks beer here – so they need someone to make sure that the beer is good quality. To do this I pour some beer on to a bench and sit in it. If my leather trousers aren't stuck to the bench in half an hour, the ale passes the test. Why? Because poor beer is very sugary and so I'd stick to the bench.

How did the Domesday Book help King William control England?

- What was the Domesday Book?
- How important is it as evidence of Norman England?

Most of us know how much money we've got. We usually know roughly how much is in our pockets or our savings accounts. We know what we own and are usually interested in what other people own too.

William the Conqueror was exactly the same – he was keen to know all about the country he had conquered and how much it was worth. In 1085 he decided to find out.

The survey

William sent officials all over England to visit each village and ask a series of detailed questions. They interviewed the priest, the steward (the man who organised the farm work in the village) and six elderly villagers.

The officials took a year to visit over 13,000 villages. Soldiers who travelled with them threatened to kill people if they didn't tell the truth. A second group visited the villages later to check they had been telling the truth.

PAUSE FOR THOUGHT

Why do you think that the officials wanted to interview the priest? Why do you think they wanted to talk to the elderly villagers too?

Source A By a monk shortly after his local village had been visited

[The official] made them search so thoroughly that there was not a single yard of land, nor even – it is a shame to tell it but he was not ashamed to do it – one ox, nor a cow, nor a swine that was not set down in his writing.

The book

All the records from the village surveys were sent to Winchester where one man copied it all together in **Latin**. The surveys filled two huge books and contained approximately two million words.

The book gave William knowledge, and knowledge was a powerful thing. It meant:

- he could work out how much each person in England could afford to pay him in taxes
- he knew exactly how many people he could get to fight for him
- he could settle any quarrels over who owned which bit of land.

However, William never got to see the finished book. While riding his horse in 1087, he slipped forward in his saddle and burst open his bladder. He died in agony. He wouldn't have been able to read it himself anyway – he couldn't read!

FACT: Winchester or Domesday?

- The book was first called the Winchester Book after the town where it was kept. After about 100 years it started to be called the Domesday Book after Doomsday – the day of judgement. Like God's judgement on you, people had no right to argue with what the book said.

The Domesday Book still survives today. It is kept in the Public Record Office in London.

Source B An English translation from the Domesday Book

At Lincoln there were 970 houses in the time of Edward the Confessor, but 166 were destroyed when the castle was built.

Source C Another extract from the Domesday Book. Birmingham is now the second-largest city in England. A furlong is about 800 metres.

Richard holds Birmingham from William. There is land for 6 ploughs; there is one plough in the demesne [lord's land]. There are 5 villeins and 4 bordars and 2 ploughs. There is a wood half a mile long and 4 furlongs broad. In the time of King Edward it was worth 20 shillings and it is still worth the same.

Source D The king owned all the land but he needed help to look after it. This diagram shows who helped the king run his country.

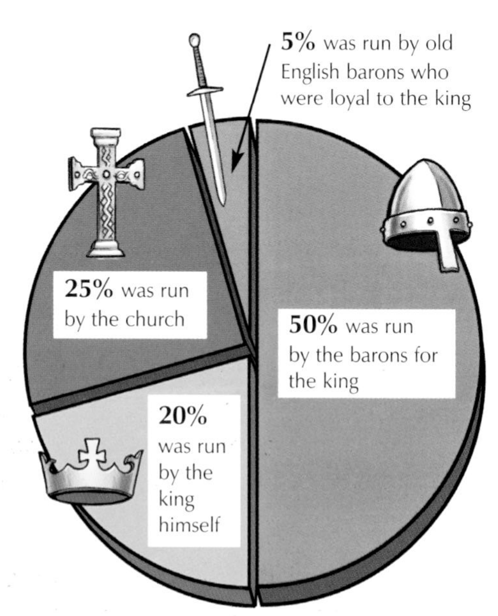

WORK

1 a Explain why the Domesday Book was made.
  b Why did it become known as the Domesday Book?

2 Read **Source A**.
  a What idea does it give us about what the survey was like for villagers?
  b Do you think the monk was happy about King William's survey or not? Explain your answer. Include any clues that might tell us how the monk felt.

3 Read **Source B**. What does the source tell us about King William's attitude towards the English?

4 According to **Sources A** and **B**, what kind of man was William?

5 What does **Source D** tell us about King William's control of his new country?

What was the feudal system and how did William use it?

AIMS
- How did the feudal system work?
- How did William use the feudal system to control the English?

Wherever we go, wherever we've been, there's usually someone in control – at home, in the classroom, at work or at a youth club. The person in charge might be a parent, a teacher or a manager. None of us lives in a world where we can do what we want when we want to. Knowing this makes the next two pages very straightforward. By the end you'll understand exactly how King William controlled England.

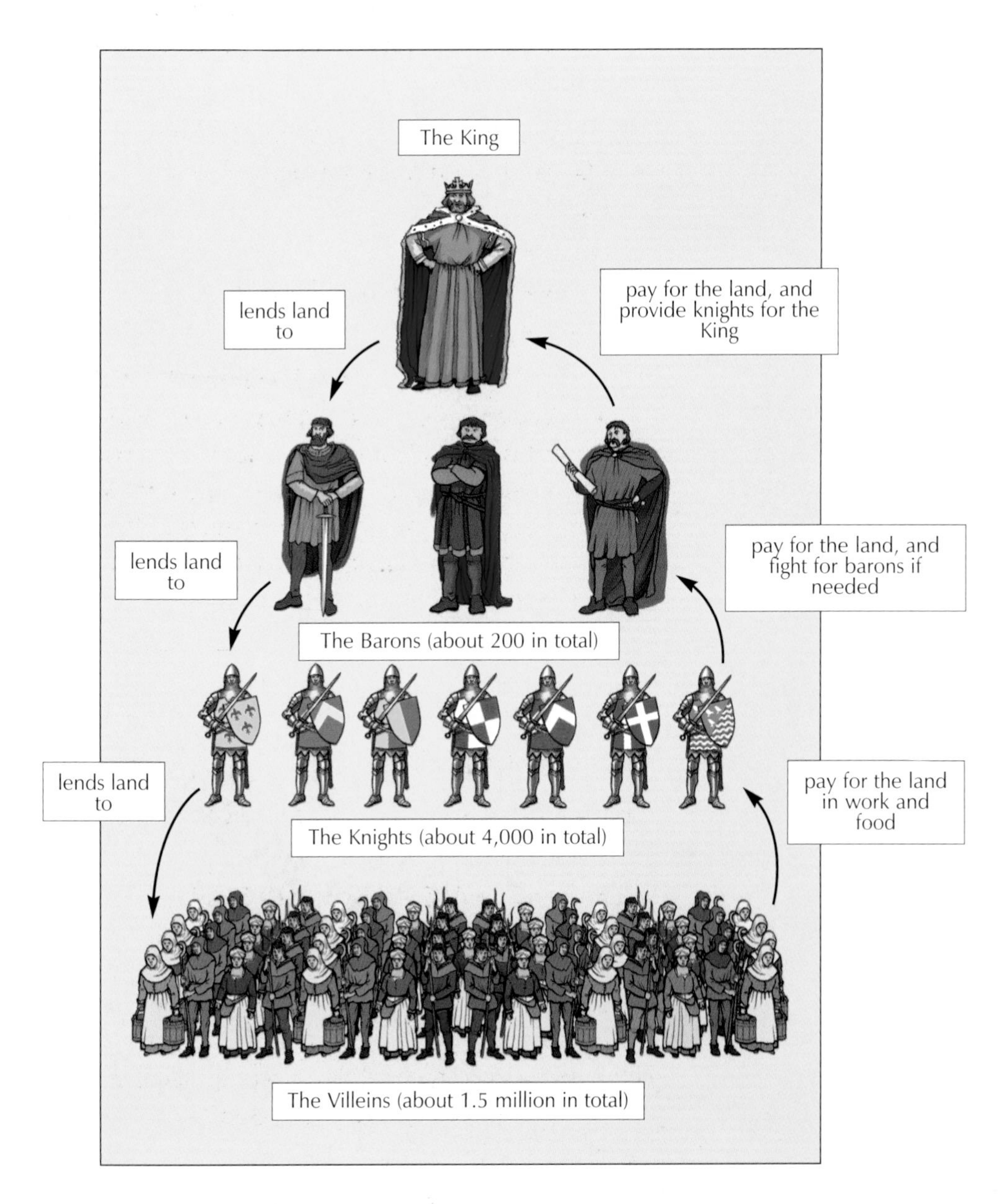

King William said that all the land in England belonged to him. But England was too large for him to manage by himself, so how did he stay in charge? His answer was to use a system of sharing out the land. The king still owned it, of course, but he could lend large areas of land to people in return for their **loyalty**.

FACT: Baron land geography

- King William didn't give his barons their land all in the same place – he carefully dotted it around England. He did this to make it difficult for the barons to build up large armies in the same area. If they became too powerful, he feared they might rebel against him.

Most of the people he gave the land to had helped him in the Battle of Hastings. He was rewarding them for helping him. 'Feudal' is the Latin word for 'land', so because the new system was based on land, it became known as the **feudal system**.

FACT: Lowest of the low

- A **villein's** life was very tough. He could never leave the lord's land (the manor) and he had to pay for practically everything. He paid to use the lord's mill, his oven and his brew house. He paid when his son was born and when his daughter got married. Even when he died, the lord was allowed to take his best animal.

Some villeins ran away, but their families were fined if they did. If the villein was caught he would be punished too. He might be lucky and avoid capture for a year and a day, and then he would be a **freeman**. The only other way of becoming a freeman was to ask the lord if you could buy your freedom.

Who was the lord?

In the Middle Ages a 'lord' was anyone above you in the feudal system. A villein had several lords, while the barons had just one – the king.

Source A ▾ A knight paying **homage** to the king. Paying homage meant that he promised to be loyal and to fight for him.

WISE UP WORDS

bailey baron besiege crenel freeman feudal system homage jester keep latin lord loyalty medieval motte rebel sappers siege villeins

WORK

1 a How did the feudal system make it easier for King William to control the English?
  b Why was William careful not to give land to his barons that was too close together?

2 a How could a lord make money from his villeins?
  b Do you think these ways of making money were fair? Explain your answer.

3 William was a clever man. As soon as he became king of England he knew he needed to do the following:
- reward his followers
- keep law and order all over England
- raise money
- find out the details of how much England was worth

  a Look at William's four needs. Which one do you think was his priority? Give reasons for your answer.
  b Divide a new page into four boxes. In the middle of each box write one of William's needs. Using words, symbols or diagrams, explain how William solved each of his needs.

Summary

- Early motte and bailey castles were replaced by stronger stone castles.
- Barons and knights used castles as bases from which to control the surrounding area.
- Stone castles were very difficult to break into, so attackers had to develop many different methods of attack.
- In 1086 William ordered a survey of all the towns in England. The information was collected in The Domesday Book.
- Everyone knew their place in the Middle Ages. It was known as the Feudal System.

HISTORY MYSTERY

How did King William II die?

It's your turn to be a history mystery detective again! This case is a rather tricky one. In fact, it is a mystery that has never been solved. See if you can piece together the clues and work out whether King William II of England was murdered or killed by accident.

The background

William the Conqueror had three sons. The eldest was named Robert, next was William and the youngest was Henry. As their father lay dying in 1087, he decided to split up his kingdom between his two eldest sons, Robert and William. Robert was to get Normandy and William was to get England. Henry got £5000.

William II became king in 1087. He was a bad-tempered, short man with red hair, which he parted down the middle. He stammered when he got angry. He became known as William 'Rufus' which is Latin for 'red' and took great care with his appearance. He always wore the most fashionable and expensive clothes.

On 1 August 1100, William Rufus travelled to the New Forest in Hampshire. He planned to go hunting for deer with his friends the next day and enjoyed a lively evening of eating, drinking and dancing. However, he didn't sleep well that night because he had a bad dream. He dreamed that something terrible was going to happen to him while out hunting. The next day he was shot and killed by an arrow through the heart. But was it an accident, or was it murder? Consider the evidence before you decide!

Evidence A

This is a version of the shooting by William of Malesbury, written in about 11

After dinner he went into the forest wi a few people, including his closest friend, Walter Tirel. Only this man stayed with him, while the others were spread out in the chase. The sun was going down, when the king let fly an arrow, slightly wounding a stag which passed in front of him; he started aft it for a long time. At this moment, Walter decided to shoot another stag which came near to him. Unable to sto it, he pierced the king's chest with arrow. The king said nothing but brok off the shaft of the arrow and fell c the wound. As a result, he died more quickly. Walter leapt on his horse ar escaped by speeding away. No one fol him. Everybody was busy with other matters.

Evidence B

Robert, Rufus's older brother, was ou the country at the time. Henry, his y brother, was hunting in the New Fores

Evidence C

This is another version of the shooting by Orderic Vitalics, written in about 1135

William sprang to his feet, mounted his horse and galloped into the wood. His brother Henry and other important men were there. They entered the wood and sent the huntsmen off into different places as usual. The king and Walter Tirel were in place in the wood with a few friends. As they waited for their prey, with their weapons ready, a beast suddenly ran between them. The king drew back from his place and Walter let fly an arrow. It sped quickly over the beast's back, grazing its hair, and wounded the king who was standing right in its path. He fell to the ground and died at once. Terrible shouts that the king was dead rang through the wood. Henry galloped atop speed to Winchester Castle where the royal treasure was.

The moment the deed was done, Tirel hurried to the coast, crossed the sea and made for his castles in France. Here, he laughed in safety at the threats of those who wanted to harm him.

Evidence D

On hearing of his brother's death, Henry rode to Winchester and got all the royal treasure. On 5 August he was crowned king of England.

Evidence E

No one at the time suggested that William's death was murder. Every writer said it was an accident. However Tirel ran away to France and never returned.

Evidence F

Robert, Rufus's older brother, arrived in England in September. Henry, the new king, threw him in prison. Robert stayed in Cardiff Castle prison until he died aged 80. He'd been in prison for over 30 years.

Evidence G

The **abbot** of Gloucester warned Rufus that he was in danger if he left his castle to go hunting. Rufus ignored him.

Evidence H

King Henry gave jobs and land to important families soon after Rufus's death, particularly to the Clare and the Giffard families.

Tirel's wife came from the Clare family and two other family members were in the hunting party on the day that Rufus died. Tirel was also related to the Giffards.

Evidence I

On his deathbed, Tirel said he had not shot the king. He even said that he wasn't there on the day that Rufus died.

WORK

To try to solve this mystery, you need to look closely at all the evidence.

1. **Find out who the suspects were.**

   Write down the names of all the people who were in the New Forest on the day William died.

2. **Find a** motive - **who might want him dead and why?**

   Who might benefit from William's death? Think about who might stand to gain the most if he died. Explain your ideas. It the motive enough to make them a murderer?

3. **Find evidence of an accident.**

   Was the death an accident? Write down any evidence you can find to support this theory.

4. **Find evidence for murder.**

   Was the death murder? Write down any evidence you can find to support this theory.

5. **Now make your decision.**

   Was William's death an accident or did someone murder him? If you believe it was an accident, write a report outlining why you think this is the case. If you think it was murder, who killed him? Write a report to outline your findings, naming the murderer and giving evidence to back up your argument.

Have you been learning?

Task 1

This is a scene from the Bayeux Tapestry. Think about the following questions before writing a description of the scene in as much detail as you can.

a What is the name of the hill?

b Which side are at the top of the hill?

c Which side are at the bottom?

d What weapons and armour does each side have?

e What happens next?

Task 2

The sources below were written about King William I. Read them carefully before answering the questions.

Source A From the *Anglo Saxon Chronicle*, a history of events written by English monks

> The king was a hard man. He took from his people much money in gold and many more hundreds of pounds in silver. This was unfair. He was very greedy. Whoever killed a deer was to be blinded. The rich complained and the poor were sad. But he did not care if everyone hated him.

Source B By a Norman monk

> The king was wiser than all the princes of his time and he was never frightened by danger. He was great in body and strong. He was a good speaker, always making it clear what he wanted. If his voice was harsh, what he said was always right for the occasion. He had been a Christian since childhood and regularly went to services each morning and evening.

a What impression of King William do we get from **Source A**? Use words from the source to help you.

b What impression of King William do we get from **Source B**? Again, use words from the source to help you.

c Why do you think it is that one source criticizes King William while the other praises him?

Task 3

The passage below doesn't make much sense. It needs capital letters, commas and full stops.

a Copy the passage, adding punctuation as you write.

stone castles were very strong a baron would spend a lot of time and money making sure that his castle was very difficult to break into sometimes the walls were over six metres thick if the people inside the castle had enough food and water they could hold out for weeks maybe even months

attackers used special weapons and tricks to get into a castle and defeat the men inside they might use a trebuchet a battering ram a mangonel or a siege tower at rochester castle in 1216 king john ordered his men to dig under the castle walls fill the tunnel with wood and set fire to it he even ordered 40 fat pigs to be thrown on to the fire the fat burned so well that one of the castle walls began to crack eventually it fell down and king john and his army stormed in

b Write a description of:
- a trebouchet
- a battering ram
- a mangonel
- a siege tower.

c Explain how, if you were inside a castle, you could defend yourself against each of the weapons in (b).

Task 4

Note-making is an important skill. To do it successfully you must pick out all the key words in the sentences. The key words are the words that are vital to the meaning of the sentence. Without these words, the sentence makes no sense.

For example, in the sentence

Harold was killed at the Battle of Hastings in 1066.

the key words are Harold, killed, Battle, Hastings, 1066.

a Write down the key words in the following sentences. These key words are your notes.
- The Domesday Book was written in 1086. It is a record of all the land in England.
- The information was collected by officials and was used to work out how much tax each person could afford to pay.
- King William also wanted to know exactly how many people he could get to fight for him.
- The Domesday Book was written in Latin.
- King William died after a riding accident so he never got to see the completed Domesday Book.

b Test your notes on a friend. They should be able to understand what you are writing about just by looking at your notes.

Task 5

Here are seven groups of words or phrases. In each group there is an odd one out. When you think you have found it, write a sentence or two to explain why you think it doesn't fit in with any of the others.

1 Duke William • Harald Hardrada • King Edward • Harold Godwinson
2 housecarl • fyrdsman • knight • local peasant
3 baron • motte • bailey • keep
4 axe • shield • sword • crossbow
5 priest • villager • king • steward
6 Normandy • England • Spain • Norway
7 portcullis • moat • hoardings • mongonel

Was religion important in medieval England?

- What was the impact of religion on everyday life?
- How could the Church use its power?

In the Middle Ages almost everyone in England believed in God, and that heaven and hell were real places. If you tried to lead a good life on earth and went to church regularly, you would probably go to heaven when you died. However, if you committed crimes, didn't pray much and were a bad person, you would face the horrors of hell.

Source A ▾ A priest describes hell

'In hell the wicked are tortured on burning trees. They were hung by the feet, or hands, or hair, or neck, or tongue, or arm. There is a horrible river, full of fish-like monsters which gobble up the souls of the wicked, who get what they deserve.'

People used religion to explain things. A broken arm or nasty infections were punishments from God. If a baby died, it was because of God's wishes. Life was hard for ordinary people, so heaven was a warm, comforting reward that made up for the suffering on earth. The people of England followed the Roman Catholic religion, led by the Pope in Rome. It was the only religion in England at this time.

The biggest building in a town or village would be the church. Unlike today, churches were very noisy places. The local church was a meeting place for people – they didn't want to spend too much time in their tiny smelly huts, with all smoke from fires and the smell of animals! Children's games, plays and summer fairs were sometimes held in the churchyard. A church was seen as a lively place, full of laughter, conversation and activity.

A village church and its priest

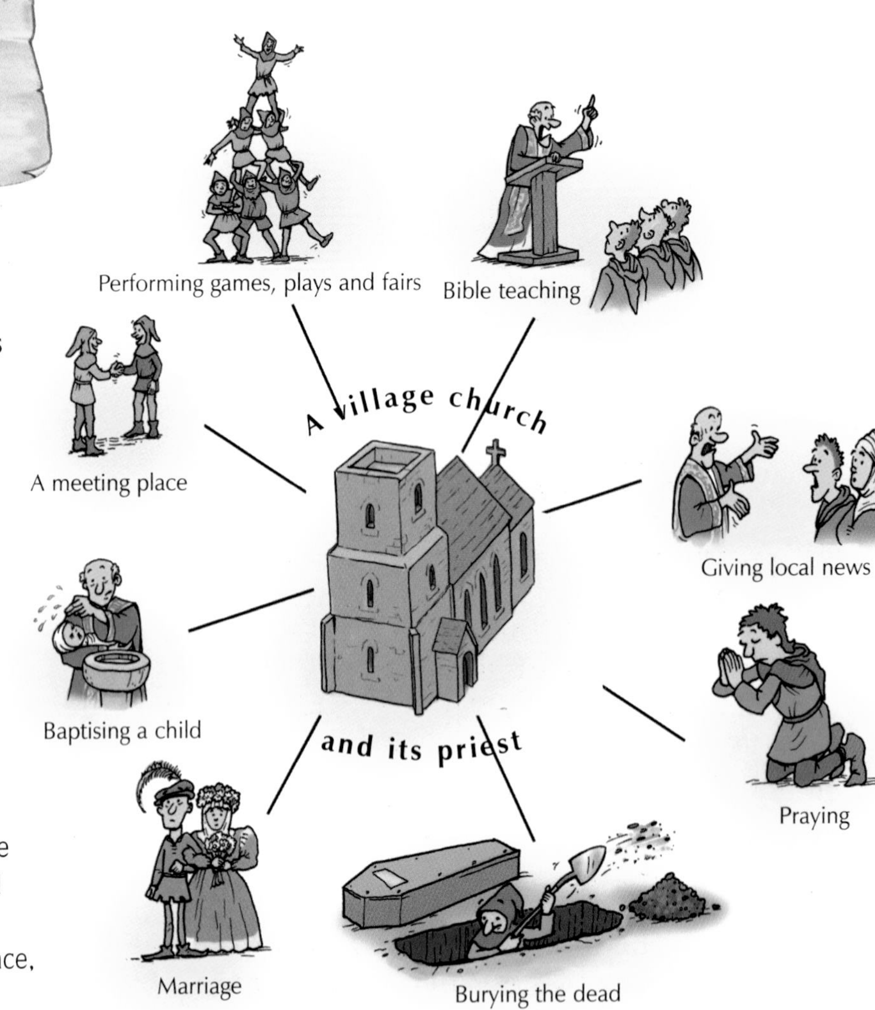

The village priest was a very important man. He cared for people from the day they were born to the day they died. He was a friend, an adviser and a local leader. During confession the priest would listen while villagers told him of the sinful things they had done.

At church services he would tell the villagers that they would go to heaven if they were good, but go to hell if they were bad. There were pictures, statues, stained glass and paintings to remind people of this. Huge doom paintings showed angels welcoming good people into heaven and devils pulling murderers into pots of boiling oil in hell. Religion was a very important part of people's lives in the Middle Ages. It gave great comfort to people whose lives were hard.

Source B ▾ A doom painting

FACT: ▸ Understanding religion

- Church services were held in Latin, so ordinary people couldn't understand them. There would be a good chance that the priest wouldn't understand much of what he was saying either. He would probably just learn the services by heart. Latin was the language of the Church, but English was the language of the people.

HUNGRY FOR MORE?

See if you can find out more about your local churches. There is a good chance that one of them was built in the Middle Ages. Visit your local library's 'local history' section or ask a librarian for advice on investigating the history of some of the medieval churches in your area.

Pay up

The villagers had to give the priest one tenth of all the food they grew. This was called the **tithe**. As you can imagine, the villagers were often unhappy about this, especially if the harvest was bad. Also, when someone died, the priest received their second-best working animal! For the peasants, worshipping God could be an expensive business.

Source C ▾ By the Bishop of Hereford in 1347. He took evidence from people as he visited the local villages.

> They say the priest was away for six weeks and made no arrangements for a substitute. He spends his time in taverns, and his tongue is loosened to the great scandal of everyone. He is living with a woman, Margaret, and he cannot read or write so cannot look after his parishioners' souls.

WORK

1 Copy and complete the following paragraph.

Everyone believed in ____________ and went to ____________ in the Middle Ages. The local church was a busy place and children's games, plays and summer ____________ were sometimes held in the ____________. People tried to lead good lives because they wanted to go to ____________. They were afraid of ________.

2 Study **Source B**.

a Why was it important to have so many pictures and paintings on church walls in the Middle Ages? Clue: Think about the language used by the priest in his services.

b What was the purpose of a doom painting? How do you think these kinds of paintings might affect the way someone behaved after leaving church?

3 a Make a list of all the ways in which a priest helped and cared for the villagers.

b According to **Source C**, how did one priest fail in his duties and upset the villagers?

A day in the life of a monk

- What was life like for medieval monks and nuns?
- What power did the Church have over people in the Middle Ages?

Some men decided to spend their whole lives worshipping God. They left their villages and went to live in the local **monastery** as monks. A monastery was a large stone building where monks would spend their days praying, working hard and caring for others. Becoming a monk meant following a strict set of rules.

The rules were written by a monk called St Benedict. They were very tough but, despite this, in 1300 there were over 12,000 monks in England. This meant that out of every 150 people who lived in England, one of them was a monk. A large monastery was called an abbey.

A boy could join a monastery if he or his parents wanted him to. He became a **novice** and some were as young as seven years of age.

Source C ▲ This is the remains of Rievaulx Abbey in Yorkshire

A good monk must:

- spend his life in service to God
- give away his property to others
- obey the abbot (the head of the monastery) at all times
- wear a **habit** (the robe) and sandals and shave the top of his head (known as a **tonsure**)
- stay in the monastery until he dies

Signature:
St Benedict

Source D By a monk from Rievaulx Abbey in 1170

> Here everything is peaceful and quiet. We are free from all the noise and worry of the world. All the monks are very friendly and no one is selfish.

FACT: Jobs for the girls

- A monastery was for men and a **nunnery** was for women. A woman who wanted to give her life to God was called a nun. Life for a nun was more or less the same as that of the monks: praying, working hard and caring for others. There were 130 nunneries in England, but only four had more than 30 nuns. Nuns were often from rich families, who paid for them to attend.

The diary of novice Arthur, aged 13¾

14 June

What a busy day! Brother Gerald woke me up at two in the morning for prayers in church. I could hardly keep awake, never mind pray for an hour. When I got back into bed at 3 o'clock I couldn't sleep because my robes were too itchy and it was freezing cold as well.

I was up again at 6 o'clock for more prayers. An hour later we had our breakfast. We eat in the refectory. It was bread and ale again; sometimes we have porridge but it is always cold and horrible. None of us is allowed to make any noise at all, not even to talk. Novice Charles isn't very good at remembering this rule, so he gets beaten a lot with the whip. He sometimes has to sleep face down because his back is cut to ribbons.

At 8 o'clock we met in the chapter house to organise work for the day. We didn't get any choice – we were just told what to do. After a short relaxing walk in the cloisters, I went off to do my morning's work in the **scriptorium**. I cut and smooth animal skins to make **vellum** to write on. I sometimes help to copy out books and decorate the capital letters and margins. At 11 o'clock we prayed again.

We ate our dinner at midday – soup, fish, bread and ale. Then there were more prayers before going out into the fields. I also spent some time in the mill today, grinding corn into flour. We're always busy here. Although our first duty is to God, our second duty is to help local people. Not all of them can afford a doctor so we provide basic free care for the sick - herbal medicines, rest and a meal. We also teach a few of the local children in our small school, provide shelter to travellers and collect clothing, food and money for the poor.

I didn't feel too well this afternoon so I called into the **infirmary**. Brother John told me to chew some poppy seeds to relieve my aching head.

We prayed again at 6 o'clock before eating our supper. Only bread and water for me, because Brother Gerald didn't think I had worked very hard. After supper we prayed again.

I've just polished my **tonsure** with a piece of stone. I must keep it free of hair – I don't want to get whipped. It's 9 o'clock and I'm about to blow out the candle in my dormitory. I have to be awake again at 2 o'clock in the morning.

WORK

1 Read the diary of novice Arthur, and then answer the following questions.

a At what time did Arthur:
- get up for prayers?
- go to sleep at night?

b In what ways did monks in monasteries try to help local people? Why do you think they did this?

c Describe what went on in the refectory, scriptorium and infirmary.

d Name two types of punishment Arthur may have received in the monastery.

2 Being a monk or a nun seems like a hard life to people today. Try to explain why you think it was that so many people chose to lead this kind of life in the Middle Ages.

WISE UP WORDS

infirmary monastery novice nunnery scriptorium tonsure vellum tithe

Summary

- Religion was part of everybody's life.
- The priest was a very important man in the village, and the church was probably the biggest building.
- Monks and nuns gave up their everyday life to dedicate themselves to God.

King Henry II and Thomas Becket: Murder in mind?

AIMS
- What was the relationship between King Henry II and Thomas Becket?
- Why did the Church and the crown come into conflict?

On 29 December 1170, four knights burst into Canterbury Cathedral and murdered Thomas Becket, the most important Church leader in England. After one knight had cut off the top of his head, another stood on Becket's neck and scattered his brains all over the floor. The knights said they were acting on the orders of King Henry II. How could this happen?

Best of friends

King Henry II and Thomas Becket used to be good friends. They hunted, got drunk and chased women together. They both enjoyed expensive clothes, magnificent palaces and fabulous food and wine. Henry even gave Becket an important job, **Chancellor** of England. The Chancellor had to be trusted by the king because he was in charge of writing the king's letters and sending out his orders.

The two men seemed to work well together and King Henry was a popular ruler. However, he had one big fault: temper tantrums. When he got angry his big grey eyes went bloodshot and flashed like lightning. King Henry once got so angry that he took off all his clothes, threw himself to the floor, and started chewing pieces of straw.

Worst enemies

In 1162 Henry gave Becket a very important new job. He was made **Archbishop** of Canterbury, placing him in charge of religion in England. We know how important religion was in the Middle Ages, so this was a very powerful position.

Henry thought he was being clever. He wanted to make some changes to the way the Church punished those priests who broke the law. He felt that Church courts were letting priests get away with crimes too easily. Church courts were separate from the king's courts and dealt with all the crimes committed by people who worked in churches. Henry thought that by putting Becket in charge of religion, Becket would then allow Henry to change the Church courts. But he was wrong!

Becket took his new job seriously. He stopped getting drunk, chasing women and wearing fancy clothes. He started to wear an itchy, goat's-hair shirt, full of fleas. He became very religious, praying for hours every day. Henry and Becket quarrelled. The king wanted to make changes in the Church but Becket refused to let him. After one particularly violent disagreement, Becket fled England to France – and he didn't return for six years!

From better to worse

After six years, Henry and Becket agreed to try to work together again. Becket arrived back in England in 1170 and immediately annoyed Henry once more. Becket was furious that while he had been away other, less important, bishops had been helping the king and doing the jobs that only the Archbishop of Canterbury should have been doing. He **excommunicated** three bishops, meaning they no longer belonged to the Church. This was a terrible sentence in the Middle Ages as it meant they would go straight to hell when they died.

When Henry heard of this, he flew into one of his rages. He said: 'Is there no one who will rid me of this **turbulent** priest?' Four knights overheard this and decided that they should try to please their king. They thought that the king wanted Becket dead, so they quickly left to find him.

WORK

1. Before the four knights set out to kill Becket, the following events occurred. Write these down in the correct chronological order.
   - 5 Becket ran away to France for six years.
   - 1. Henry and Becket became best friends.
   - 4 Becket took his new job very seriously.
   - 3 Henry made Becket Archbishop of Canterbury.
   - 2. Henry made Becket Chancellor of England.
   - 7 Henry was heard to say: 'Is there no one who will rid me of this turbulent priest?'
   - 6 Becket excommunicated three bishops.
2. a Think of five words to describe King Henry II.
   b Think of five words to describe Thomas Becket.
   c Are any of your words the same? Using the words you have listed, write two paragraphs describing Henry and Becket.
3. Why do you think Henry believed making Becket Archbishop of Canterbury was such a good idea?
4. Looking back, why might making Becket Archbishop of Canterbury not have been such a good idea?

Newsflash: Murder in the cathedral!

- How was Becket murdered and by whom?
- What was Henry II's reaction to Becket's murder?

We know that there were no televisions or news programmes in the Middle Ages. But if there had been live news reports at that time, the events of 29 December 1170 might have been presented like this...

TV presenter: We're sorry to interrupt your Christmas episode of *Ye olde Coronation Street*, but amazing news has just come in. Thomas Becket, Archbishop of Canterbury, is dead. Over to Annette Ball, our reporter, live at the scene.

Live reporter: Thank you, Jill. Shocking scenes here at Canterbury Cathedral. Becket has been butchered. We can now exclusively reveal the names of the four knights who have committed this crime. We've been told that Reginald Fitzurse, William de Traci, Richard Britto and Hugh de Morville are the men in the frame. Even more shocking is that the knights have said that they were acting on the orders of King Henry II... we're not sure what to make of that news here. Back to you, Jill.

TV presenter: Were there any witnesses? Can you find any for us?

Live reporter: The knights have run away. Some people say that there was a flash of lightning and a crash of thunder as they escaped. I do have an eyewitness, Jill, his name is Edward Grim, a monk who claims to have seen it all. [To the monk] What can you tell us, Edward?

Edward Grim: It was awful, Annette. I'm shaking with fear and anger. I'm so upset... I'm going to have to write it down. The murderers came in full armour with swords and axes. The monks tried to bolt the doors to keep them out but the Archbishop ordered them to be opened, saying, 'It's not right to make a fortress of a house of prayer.' In a mad fury the knights called out, 'Where is Thomas Becket, **traitor** to the King and Country?' Becket replied, 'I'm ready to die.' They tried to drag him outside to kill him, but he clung to a pillar. Then, realising he was about to die, he bowed his head in prayer and joined his hands together.

The first blow struck his head and almost cut my arm. The second blow struck his head again but he stood firm. The third blow made him fall on his knees and elbows. The fourth blow cut the top off his head. A knight put his foot on the neck of the holy priest and scattered his blood and brains all over

the floor. Amazingly, one of my friends, William Fitzstephen, thought he saw one of the attackers put the end of his sword into Becket's skull and scoop out some of his brains. After this, one of the knights shouted, 'Let us away. This fellow will get up no more.'

Why do you think the knights tried to drag Becket outside the cathedral?

Live reporter: Incredible scenes, Jill. This news will shock the country. What will happen next? Back to you in the studio.

TV reporter: That's the big question tonight. The men claimed to be acting on King Henry's orders, but how will the king respond?

Although this news report is imaginary, the events it describes were real, using evidence available to historians. The people of England were indeed shocked by the murder – Thomas Becket had been the leader of the English Church and now he lay dead on his cathedral floor.

What happened to Henry II?

Becket was buried in Canterbury Cathedral and Henry II took the blame for his murder. To show how sorry he was, he walked through the streets of Canterbury with no shoes on. He allowed monks to whip him and he spent the night lying on the floor near Becket's tomb.

What happened to the knights

They didn't last long! King Henry sent them on a **pilgrimage** to the Holy Land, and they all died on the journey.

After the murder

Soon after the murder, people started to report that miracles were happening to people after they had visited Becket's grave. Blind people claimed that they could see, the crippled that they could walk and the deaf that they could hear. In 1173 Becket was made a saint by the Pope. Soon, thousands of **pilgrims** were going on pilgrimages to the tomb of Saint Thomas Becket.

WISE UP WORDS

archbishop chancellor excommunicated pilgrimage pilgrims traitor turbulent

WORK

1 Who do you think was to blame for Becket's death – was it Becket himself, King Henry or the knights, or was it a combination of them all? Explain your answer.

2 Design a front page for a newspaper article reporting the shocking events of 29 December 1170. Try to include the following details:
- an eye-catching headline
- details of the main events
- eyewitness accounts – quotes from Edward Grim perhaps.
- a picture from the scene of the crime
- the king's immediate reaction, e.g. a brief interview.

3 Why do you think King Henry allowed monks to whip him?

Summary

- King Henry II and Thomas Becket argued over who controlled the Church
- Henry lost his temper and four knights decided to kill Becket to please their King
- Becket was murdered in Canterbury Cathedral

What were the Wars of the Cross?

- Why did people want to join the crusade?
- When did the four main Crusades take place?

The people of Europe all had one thing in common – their religion. They were all Christians and their religious leader on earth was the Pope.

For medieval Christians, Jerusalem was the most important city on earth. Jesus had lived there, and was crucified and buried there. Naturally, Christians wanted to visit Jerusalem to say they had been to a place so important in the life of Jesus. These travellers were known as pilgrims. They also enjoyed visiting places linked to the life of Jesus. The whole area became known as the Holy Land.

This area was an important place for **Muslims** too. Their great leader, the **Prophet** Muhammad, is said to have visited heaven from Jerusalem. In 1070 Arab Muslims controlled the Holy Land and allowed Christians to visit freely. However, things were about to change.

A fierce fighting tribe from the east called the **Turks** took over Jerusalem and the Holy Land. These Turks were also Muslims, but they believed that no one but Muslims should set foot in the Holy Land. Christians who returned home from the Holy Land told stories of how they had been beaten and tortured by the Turks. Some pilgrims were even killed. In 1096 Pope Urban II urged all kings, lords, soldiers and ordinary people to go and fight the Muslim Turks. He promised that anyone who died fighting would go straight to heaven. Thousands of people decided to go. They sewed crosses, the sign of Christianity, on to their clothes. These journeys became known as the **Crusades**, which means 'Wars of the Cross'. Between 1100 and 1250 there were seven Crusades against the Muslim Turks.

Source B ▾ Pope Urban II urged Christians to go and fight the Muslim Turks

> The Turks, a race alien to God, have invaded the land of the Christians. They slaughter and capture many. They tear out their organs and tie them to a stake. They tie some to posts and shoot them full of arrows. They cut off their heads. The days of the Devil are here.

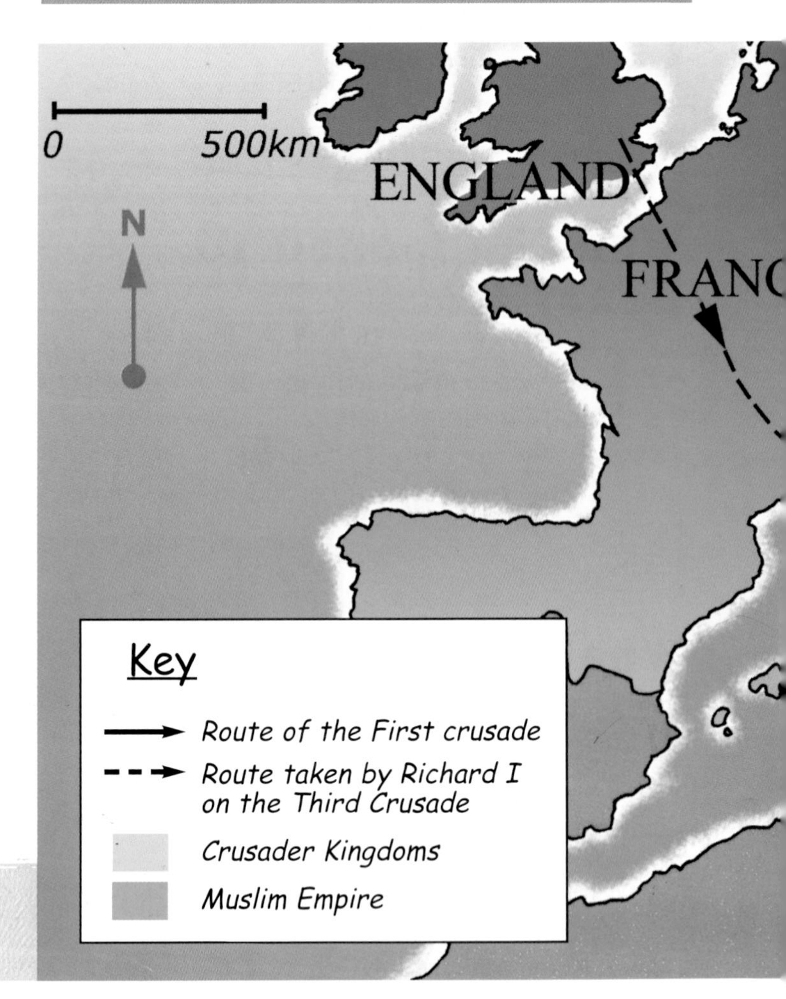

Source A ▸ The routes taken by those on the First and the Third Crusade

The First Crusade

Date: 1097.

Leader: Robert of Normandy, son of William the Conqueror.

Who took part?: Mainly well-trained, well-armed French knights.

What happened?: They travelled 1,500 miles and were exhausted when they got to the Holy Land. Many died from disease as well as fighting. Battles were won at Nicaea, Antioch and they finally captured Jerusalem in July 1099.

Result: A Christian victory. Jerusalem stayed in Christian hands for over 80 years. Some Christians built castles and settled in the Holy Land. A group of fighting monks, the Knights Templar, stayed in the Holy Land to protect Christians.

The People's Crusade

Date: 1096.

Leader: A monk called Peter the Hermit.

Who took part?: A few thousand peasants, including some knights, women and children.

What happened?: The 'army' was poorly trained, had few proper weapons and was soon short of food. After a long and dangerous journey to the Holy Land, they were slaughtered by the Muslim Turks.

Result: An easy Muslim victory

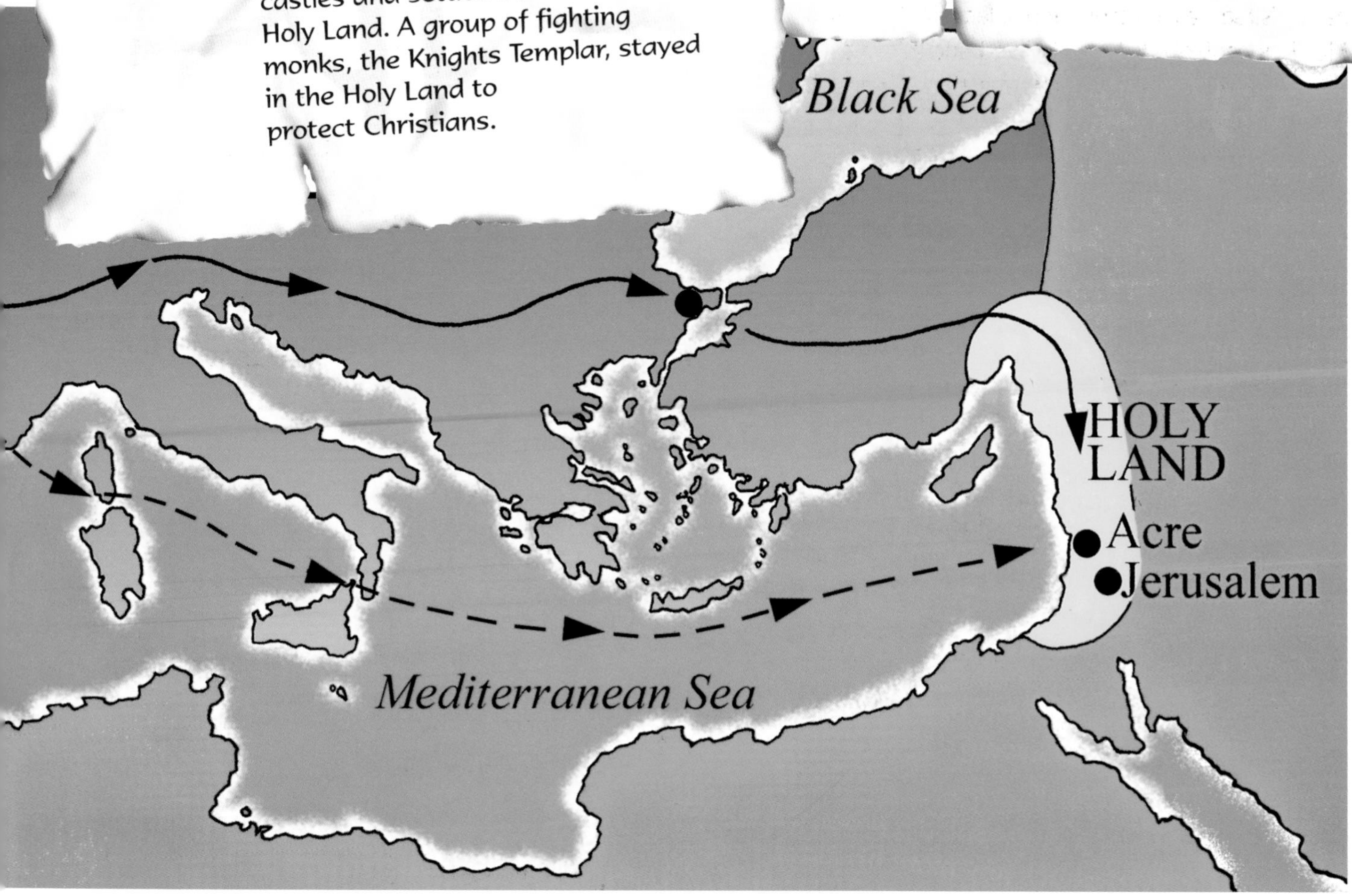

Source C ◂ A 14th century illustration of Saladin's army

The Second Crusade

Date: 1147.

Leader: Emperor Conrad of Germany and King Louis VII of France.

Who took part?: Well-armed German and French knights. They went in an attempt to win back some of the land the Turks had taken.

What happened?: Christian Crusaders were heavily defeated at Damascus.

Result: The Crusade was abandoned. The Turks kept hold of the land. By 1187 Jerusalem had been recaptured by the Turks.

The Third Crusade

Date: 1189.

Leader: Richard I, king of England ('the Lionheart'), Phillip of France and Emperor Frederick of Germany. The Muslim Turks (now known as Saracens) were led by Saladin, a brilliant soldier.

Who took part?: The Christian Crusaders were well armed and trained.

What happened?: Saladin and the Saracens had taken over Jerusalem again. The Christians tried to win it back. Frederick drowned while crossing a river but his men decided to pickle his body in vinegar and take it with them. Richard and Phillip, the two other leaders, spent most of their time arguing. Soon after capturing a town called Acre near Jerusalem, Phillip returned home. Richard and Saladin agreed to make peace.

Result: A draw. Saladin promised not to attack any more hristians who wanted to visit the Holy Land.

FACT: Cruel crusades

- A crusader called Robert was captured by Atabeg of Damascus, a fierce Turk. Robert was beheaded, his body fed to the dogs, and his skull used as a drinking cup!

There were other Crusades as well as those listed here. Some Crusaders never managed to get anywhere near the Holy Land; others did but were either killed by illness or in battle. The great period of the Crusades finally ended in 1291 when the Muslims captured the last Christian town of Acre and slaughtered every Christian they could find. After nearly 200 years of trying, the Christian Crusaders had failed to take and keep control of the Holy Land.

Crusaders who died abroad didn't want to be buried in Muslim soil so they left instructions for their bodies to be sent home if they died. However, the journey home was long and the bodies would go mouldy. The solution was simple and hygienic: bodies were boiled in a big tub of oil, the flesh was removed and the bones were sent home.

Source D ▸ A Crusader's tomb

WORK

1 Write a sentence to explain each of the following words.
pilgrim • Holy Land • Turks • Crusade

2 Why were Jerusalem and the Holy Land so important to both Muslims and Christians?

3 Read **Source B**.
  a What strong words does Pope Urban II use to show how he feels about the Turks?
  b Why do you think Urban used such strong language?

4 a Make a large copy of the following timeline.

1080 1100 1120 1140 1160 1180 1200 1220 1240 1260 1280 1300

  b On your timeline, label all the major events you have read about in this section. For example, '1096: Pope Urban II calls for the First Crusade.'

In 1212 there was a Children's Crusade. Thousands of boys and girls followed a 12 year-old French shepherd boy called Stephen on a journey to the Holy Land. It was a tragic story as only one child ever returned home. Find out more about it: an internet search using the terms "Hugh the Iron" and "William the Pig" might help …

Match of the day

AIMS
- Why was the Battle of Jaffa in 1192 so important?
- How was each side equipped for the battle?

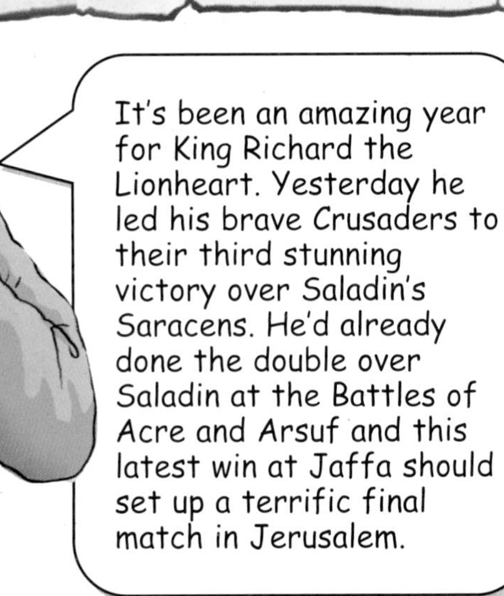

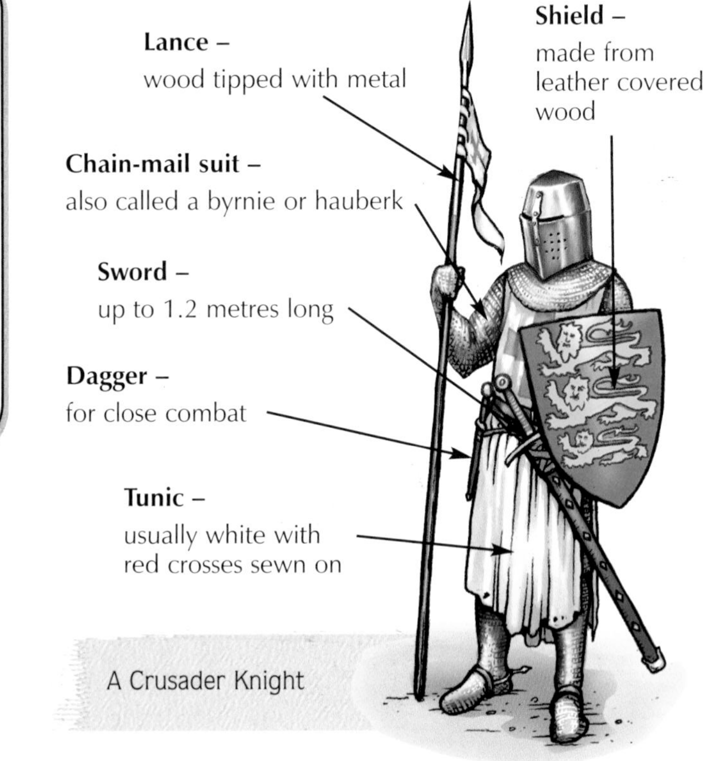

A Crusader Knight

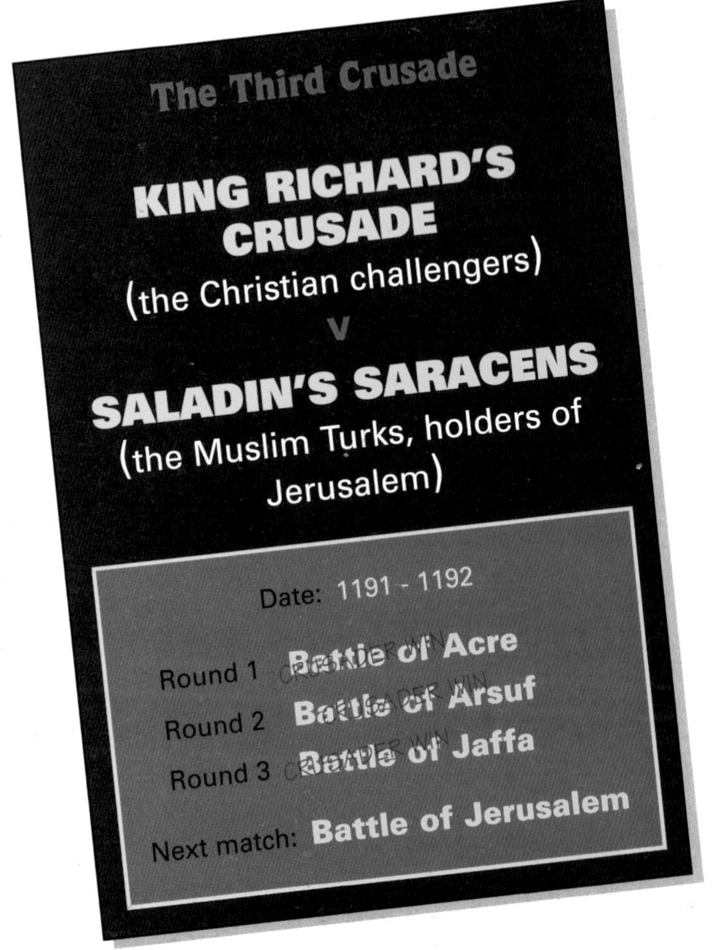

*Why do you think the knight wore a white **tunic** over his chain mail? Clue: What was the climate in the Holy Land?*

The Battle of Jaffa

On 5 August 1192 Saladin's army of 7,000 men ambushed King Richard's men. Richard had about 2,000 foot soldiers and archers and about 54 knights. His knights had only 15 horses between them as many had been killed in previous battles at Acre and Arsuf.

King Richard ordered his men to form a semi-circle and face the Saracens. They hammered long sticks into the ground in the hope of stabbing enemy horses when they charged. The Saracens attacked about seven times, but each time they were forced to fall back. They couldn't break through the line to kill King Richard. Each time the Saracens retreated they were fired upon by Richard's archers.

Eventually Saladin decided to retreat and fled towards nearby Jerusalem. Amazingly, King Richard's small army had won the day. They decided to attack Jerusalem next.

Let's have another look at Saladin's boys, a fearsome bunch of Turks who haven't performed well lately. They've lost three in a row now and their brilliant leader Saladin will be hoping that this loss of form won't continue in Jerusalem.

Helmet – did not cover all the face, but was worn with a coif - a chain mail hood

Al-qutum – padded shirt or tunic

Shield – round wooden shield with a metal rim

Bow and arrows – a Saracen was trained to fire arrows as he rode his horse

Swords – broad-bladed chopping sword, sometimes called a falchion

A Muslim Saracen

What happened next?

Jerusalem was still controlled by Saladin and the Muslim Saracens. He knew Richard would head there next after his victory at Jaffa. However, just as Richard got close to Jerusalem, he received bad news from England. His brother John was plotting to seize the crown and Richard decided to return home. He was also ill from his wounds. On 2 September he met with Saladin and worked out a deal. Jerusalem would remain in Saracen hands but Christians could visit there without coming to any harm. In October 1192 King Richard the Lionheart and his Crusaders left the Holy Land.

After the Battle of Acre Richard's men killed over 3000 Saracens, including women and children. However, he kept some prisoners alive in case the army ran short of food on the way to Jerusalem... the Crusaders could eat the prisoners!

FACT: The long road home

- On his way back to England in 1192, King Richard was taken prisoner and held to **ransom** in Austria. After the English paid a fortune for his return, Richard finally made it home in 1194. In total, King Richard spent about six months of his ten-year reign in the country he ruled.

WORK

1 Match up the words on the left with the correct description on the right.

Lance	A padded shirt worn underneath chain mail.
Al-qutum	A long heavy weapon. It needed two hands to lift it.
Crusader sword	A Saracen sword.
Tunic	A long wooden spear, tipped with steel.
Falchion	Worn over chain mail, usually showing a red cross.

2 Some historians have called King Richard's victory at the Battle of Jaffa a 'surprise win'. Why do you think it has been called this? Give reasons for your answer.

3 Jerusalem was the most important city in the Holy Land. Why didn't King Richard try to capture it when he had the chance?

4 Why was Richard away from England for so much of his reign? What does this tell us about the qualities of medieval kings?

Franks and Saracens: What did they think of each other?

- What did Christians think of Muslims, and what did Muslims think of Christians?
- Did they learn anything from each other?

The Crusaders used the word '**Saracens**' to describe all Muslims in the Holy Land. Muslims used the word '**Franks**' to describe all Crusaders. The Crusades were known as a 'holy war' because each side was fighting for what they believed their God wanted.

So what did they think of each other? The following sources were written by either Christians or Muslims.

Source E

If they thought that a Christian had eaten gold or silver to hide it they forced them to vomit or tear open their stomachs with a blade to reveal the secret.

Source G

Saladin thought of nothing but the holy war. He did not spend a single gold coin on anything else. He made sure that his men were fed and cared for. He never said bad things about people.

Source F

A man was accused of a crime, so they dropped him in water. Their idea was that if he was innocent he would sink, but if he was guilty he would float. This man did his best to sink but he could not do it. He was found guilty and they pierced his eyes with red hot metal - may Allah's curse be upon them.

Source H

Saladin devoted much of his time to drinking and gambling. He took over countries by force and trickery. This greedy tyrant then took the Holy Land.

Source I

> The Franks only study war, so have large bodies but small minds. I want my son to study science, literature, algebra, philosophy, music, history and medicine. He will not do this in Europe.

Source J

> Count Robert was captured near Damascus. His head was cut off and his body was thrown to the dogs. His skull was used as a drinking cup and was covered in jewels.

Source K

> These people study no science and are more like animals than human beings. Those who live in England are so far away from the sun that they have become stupid.

The Crusaders and the Saracens did not fight all the time. There were long periods when they held a **truce** and were able to mix and learn from each other. Without a doubt, the Crusaders learned the most:

Language

- The Crusaders started to use Arabic words such as sugar, arsenal, syrup, lemon, admiral and algebra

New Products

- The Crusaders brought back many goods that we take for granted today – lemons, melons, apricots, cotton, spices (nutmeg, cinnamon), slippers, glass mirrors

Knowledge

- The Crusaders learned about:
  - science (magnetic compass)
  - medicine (treating injuries better)
  - geography (map making)
  - mathematics (new number system)

Fighting and castle building

- The Saracens used archers a lot
- Europeans, especially the English, started to train archers in huge numbers
- The Saracens also built better castles using a whole series of strong round towers joined by a thick wall
- Many knights copied these castles when they got home

WISE UP WORDS

crusades franks hermit muslims prophet ransom saracens truce tunic turks

Summary

- Christians and Muslims fought during the Crusades for control of Jerusalem and the Holy Land.
- After nearly 200 years of fighting, the Muslims kept the Holy Land.
- Some of the things the Crusaders learned in the Holy Land were very important.

WORK

1. Read through **Sources E** to **K** and, for each one, try to work out whether it was written by a Crusader or a Saracen. Give reasons for your answers.
2. If you were trying to find out about the Crusades, why would it be a bad idea just to read stories written by a Christian Crusader?
3. Look at the spider diagram above. You will see that the Crusaders learned a lot from the Saracens. Design a poster to show what the Crusaders learned and brought back from the Holy Land. You cannot use more than 15 words on your poster, but someone reading it should be able to understand the importance of the Crusades.

Were all medieval monarchs successful?

- What were the key qualities of medieval kings?
- What was the Magna Carta and why was it important?

The king's role was often difficult: keeping law and order, making England safe from attack, raising armies and collecting taxes. Sensible kings asked for help from powerful friends like barons and bishops. Sometimes the king didn't rule his kingdom very well and the barons rebelled against him. This section looks at two kings who made mistakes in the way they ruled and how England changed as a result. Some of these changes are still around today.

King John (1199–1216) 'Magna Carta Man'

Family background: Son of Henry II, younger brother of crusading King Richard I ('the Lionheart'). Actually, King John was unlucky in that when he became king in 1199 his older brother had spent a fortune fighting the Crusades. King John's treasury was almost empty.

Mistake no. 1: **He lost wars**. John fought against his great rival, the king of France, and lost. John lost Normandy, Anjou and Maine - all areas of France that his father had ruled. Some people nicknamed him 'Lackland' because he lacked land. Others called him 'Softsword'.

Mistake no. 2: **He upset the Pope**. The Pope usually chose bishops and archbishops but King John wanted to do this instead. The Pope refused and John banned him from England. The Pope was very angry and closed all the churches for seven years. No one could get married or buried properly.

Mistake no. 3: **He asked for high taxes**. King John demanded that his barons provided either soldiers to fight for him or money instead. The barons were furious, asking why they should supply men or money to such a bad soldier and king. King John even ordered sons to a pay tax when their fathers died. He charged one man £600, a fortune in those days.

Mistake no. 4: **He didn't treat people very well**. King John could be cruel. He treated the monks badly and once threw some blind and crippled monks out of a monastery. In 1203 he murdered his nephew Arthur in a drunken rage. According to one monk,

'John became drunk and murdered him with his own hand; and tying a heavy stone to the body, threw it into a river.'

By 1215 the barons decided they'd had enough. They gave John a choice - to change his policies and the way the country was managed, or they'd fight him. They listed their demands and marched towards London to present them to the king. The list became known as the Magna Carta (meaning 'Great **Charter**') and contained 63 clauses or rights that the barons thought they should have.

In June 1215 the barons met the king in a field at Runnymede, beside the River Thames. Some barons didn't turn up, fearing the king might be preparing a trap to capture and execute them. They needn't have worried. After some days of discussions, King John sealed the Magna Carta to show he agreed – he couldn't write, so he couldn't sign it.

At the time the Magna Carta was seen as something of a failure. King John was soon saying he had been bullied into agreeing to it and the barons were accused of being selfish and looking after themselves. After all, the Magna Carta didn't apply to peasants, only to free rich men like the barons.

However, King John died in 1216 and, in the years that followed, the Magna Carta became more and more important. It introduced the idea that there are some laws that even the king must accept. The Magna Carta meant that the king had to ask the advice of the barons and bishops.

Some of the laws are still important to us today, such as:

- we cannot be punished without a fair trial
- we cannot be taxed unfairly.

America copied part of our Magna Carta. Part of their constitution written in 1776 reads:

"no person shall be held to answer for a crime without trial by jury nor shall their life, liberty or property be taken without following the law."

Remember what you read at the start of these pages? "Bad" King John changed things forever.

MAGNA CARTA 1215: THE MAIN BITS!

I, King John accept that I have to run my country according to the law. I agree:

1. not to interfere with the Church
2. not to imprison nobles without a trial
3. that trials will be held quickly and fairly
4. to stop unfair taxes
5. that I will not ask for extra taxes
6. to let Merchants travel around the country to buy and sell without having to pay large taxes

King John couldn't read or write, so he stamped Magna Carta with his seal

WORK

1. King John upset a lot of people. Make a list of all these people, and then explain how he upset them.
2. Think of three words that best describe King John. Say why you chose them.
3. a Make a list of the main points in the Magna Carta.
   b Which of the points are still important today?
4. a Discuss with your teacher the difference between the words short-term and long-term.
   b Was the Magna Carta a short-term or a long-term success? Explain your answer.
5. Draw up your own Magna Carta for your school. List at least six changes you would like to see. For every change you must explain your reasons behind it. Remember that schools are here to educate young people, so each change should help your education.

PAUSE FOR THOUGHT

As a human being you have certain rights. For example, in this country children have the right to 'free education'. Can you spot any of your 'rights' in the Magna Carta?

Long live the king?

- Why was King Henry III so unpopular?
- How did the barons try to improve things?
- How did England get its first parliament?

King John died in 1216. His son Henry was only nine years old when he became King Henry III of England. As you would expect, the young king needed help. The advice he received, however, wasn't always wise and most of it came from friends and relations of his wife, Eleanor. As a, result the English barons were soon not happy again and they decided to rebel.

Henry III (1216-1272) 'Hopeless Henry'

Family background: Son of King John. His wife, Eleanor, wasn't very popular because she made Henry give the best jobs to her friends and family. Once she was pelted with rubbish when she arrived in London. Henry put her in the Tower of London for her own protection.

Mistake no. 1: **He lost wars**. Henry wasn't a very good soldier. He tried hard to win back some of the land that his father had lost during his reign, but failed.

Mistake no. 2: **His wife**. Eleanor begged Henry to give the Archbishop of Canterbury's job to her uncle. He did. This wasn't a popular move with many monks.

Mistake no. 3: **He asked for high taxes**. Wars were expensive and the king kept taking huge taxes from the people to pay for them. He even wasted money trying to buy the island of Sicily for his younger son Edmund!

Mistake no. 4: **He didn't treat people very nicely**. King Henry annoyed the monks because he gave the Archbishop of Canterbury's job to his wife's uncle. He also regularly received a gift of £100 from the people of London. After a few years he stopped thanking them as he started to take it for granted. When the Londoners complained, he still didn't care.

By 1258 the barons had had enough. They were fed up with King Henry III. Seven of the most angry barons met the king at Oxford and told him to sign the Provisions of Oxford, a document that gave much of the king's power to the barons. Reluctantly, the king signed but his furious young son Prince Edward wanted revenge.

In 1264 the barons and the king's army fought each other at the Battle of Lewes in Sussex. The barons were led by Simon de Montfort, the King's brother-in-law. They beat King Henry's army and took him and his son Edward prisoner. Simon decided that the king had made too many mistakes and needed some help and advice, so in 1265 he set up the first **parliament**.

The first parliament

The king met with important people in Parliament to discuss how best to run the country. Parliament comes from the French word 'parler' which means 'to talk'. Kings had been asking for advice for years, but Simon de Montfort's parliament was different. As well as the usual rich, important lords (the barons and bishops), he invited two knights from each county and two important men from large towns. These knights and townsmen became known as the commoners, and later the **Commons**.

For the first time, ordinary people in the form of the townsmen had some say in the way in which England was run. Peasants still weren't included, but the first parliament was an important breakthrough. The Lords and Commons officially helped the king to run the country and met in separate houses. The British Parliament, made up of the House of Lords and the House of Commons, still meets like this today.

Source A ▲ A medieval document showing a diagram of King Edward I's parliament

Simon de Montfort's fate

De Montfort didn't last long. Prince Edward escaped from prison and defeated Simon's army at Evesham in August 1265. Simon's body was cut to pieces. His testicles were cut off and hung around his nose. His head was sent as a present to a baron who hated him.

What happened to parliament?

Prince Edward became King Edward I after his father's death, in 1272 and he continued to meet with parliament. Parliament soon realised their power. If the king needed money (and often he did), he needed parliament to get it for him. In return Parliament might ask the king for permission to build a new port or introduce new laws about food or cloth. Although it couldn't tell the king what to do, Parliament became a powerful force in England.

FACT: Language change

- Parliament started to use English, rather than French, during the 1300s. The English were fighting the French so much that it didn't seen right to talk about England using the enemy's language.

WORK

1 What made Henry so unpopular with his barons?

2 Explain the importance of the following dates.

1216 • 1258 • 1264 • 1265

3 a Who was Simon de Montfort?

b What powers did the first parliament have?

4 a Which types of people were invited to join the first parliament in 1265?

b Why was this such an important change in the way that England was ruled?

King Edward I: 'The bully boy'

AIMS ▸ What is the history of conflict between England, Wales and Scotland?

King Edward I was the son of a weak king, Henry III, who had ruled England badly. Edward was determined to be a strong monarch and a powerful soldier. He would show his power by beating the troublesome Welsh and the awkward Scots.

Source B ▲ Conwy Castle, built in 1283 by King Edward's favourite builder Master James of St George

King Edward started by attacking Wales. In 1277 he marched a huge army into Wales with the aim of capturing the welsh leader, a powerful prince called Llywelyn. Besieged and without food Llywelyn gave in and promised to obey King Edward at all times. He didn't keep his promise. Four years later he and his brother Daffyd started fighting the English again. Llywelyn was eventually killed in battle and his head stuck on a spike on top of the Tower of London. In 1283 Daffyd was captured, hung and cut into pieces. The different parts of his body were sent to different English cities. His head was stuck on a spike next to his brother's. His sons were thrown in jail in Bristol and his daughters were forced to be nuns.

Throughout his reign Edward built a string of castles to keep the Welsh under control. He also introduced a new tradition that still survives to this day. He gave his baby son the title Prince of Wales so that no Welsh prince could claim the title for himself. Ever since, the English ruler's eldest son has been given this title.

FACT: ▸ The true Prince of Wales

- The Welsh continued to fight the English. In 1400 a Welshman called Owen Glyndwr (pronounced Glendower) led his countrymen into battle again. He was defeated but never captured and hid in the mountains. No one knows to this day when he died or where he is buried.

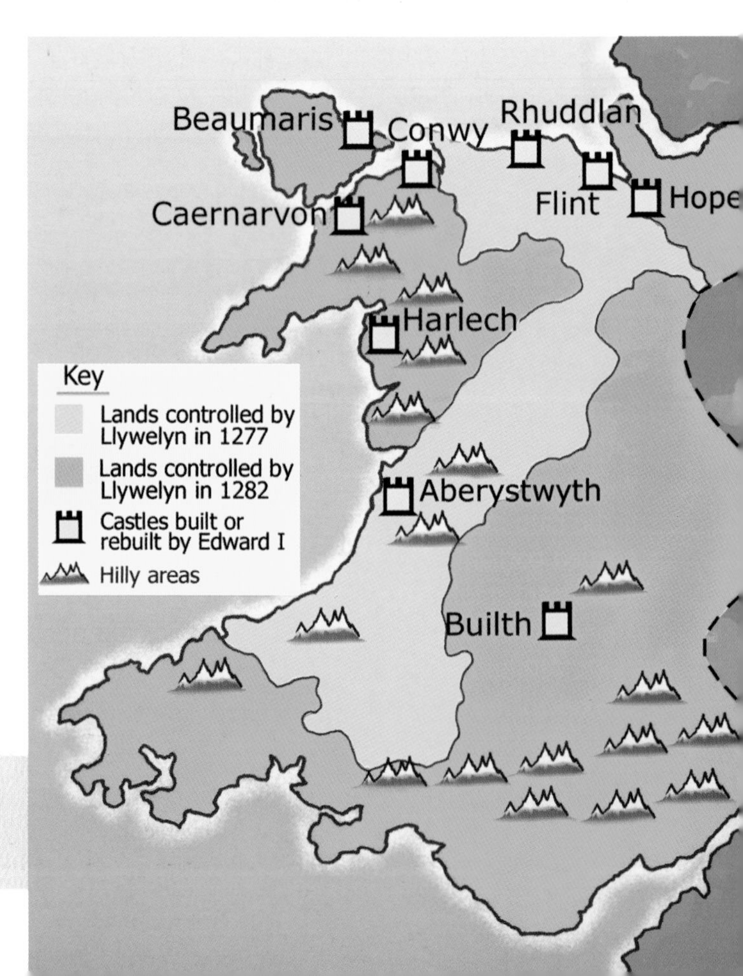

Source C ▸ Map of Wales showing the rise of Llywelyn and castles built by Edward I

Edward wanted to control Scotland as well as Wales. In 1290 he was asked to choose the next Scottish king when the old King Alexander III died. Edward chose John Balliol but forced him to make a promise. Balliol was allowed to be the new ruler of Scotland, but he had to obey Edward at all times. Balliol agreed because he was keen to be the new ruler at any cost.

Once in power, Balliol soon changed his mind and wanted to have complete control of Scotland himself. Edward decided to teach Balliol and the Scots a lesson. He gathered a massive army in Newcastle and marched into Scotland. In 1296 Balliol was captured and thrown into prison. Like Wales, Scotland was now under Edward's control.

However, when Edward returned to England the Scots rose up in **rebellion**. Their new leader was William Wallace and they defeated the English in a famous battle at Stirling Bridge in 1297. Wallace skinned one of the men he killed and turned his skin into a sword belt. Edward returned to Scotland the following year and defeated the Scots at the Battle of Falkirk. Wallace was captured in 1305 and suffered the terrible fate of death by hanging, drawing and quartering. His head was put on a spike and placed on London Bridge. An arm and a leg were each sent to Perth, Aberdeen, Newcastle and Berwick.

PAUSE FOR THOUGHT

If someone rebelled against King Edward, he punished them in a horrific way and put their body parts on public display in different parts of the country. Why do you think he did this?

WISE UP WORDS

charter commons parliament rebellion

Robert Bruce

In 1306 the Scots found a new leader in Robert Bruce. Edward once again marched north to invade Scotland, but he died on the journey. He was 68 years old and left clear instructions as to what he wanted written on his grave. His tomb in Westminster Abbey in London reads, 'Here is Edward I, the Hammer of the Scots: keep my faith.'

King Edward's son was also called Edward. He was crowned King Edward II in 1307. He wasn't a particularly good soldier and Robert Bruce took full advantage of this. In June 1314 Edward II sent a huge army of over 25,000 men to Scotland to fight Robert Bruce and his army of 7000. At Bannockburn the Scots defeated the English in just one day.

Robert Bruce remained King of Scotland whilst Edward II and his battered and bruised army returned to England. Scotland remained a seperate country, not tied to England at all for the next 300 years.

*Mel Gibson played William Wallace in the film **Braveheart**. Some historians criticised it because they said that it wasn't true to life. There are many things that were added to the story. Try to find out what parts of the story were changed.*

WORK

1. Why was Edward I later given the nickname "Hammer of the Scots"?
2. Which of these words do you think best describes Edward I:
   cruel, weak, clever, powerful, aggressive, blood-thirsty, kind, stupid
   Explain your choice of words.
3. Why do you think Edward I was so determined to control Wales and Scotland?

We're all going to die...

▸ What were the symptoms and effects of the Black Death?

In 1348 the people of England were gripped by fear. A killer **plague** was spreading across the country and no one could stop it. Who would be next? The Black Death had arrived...

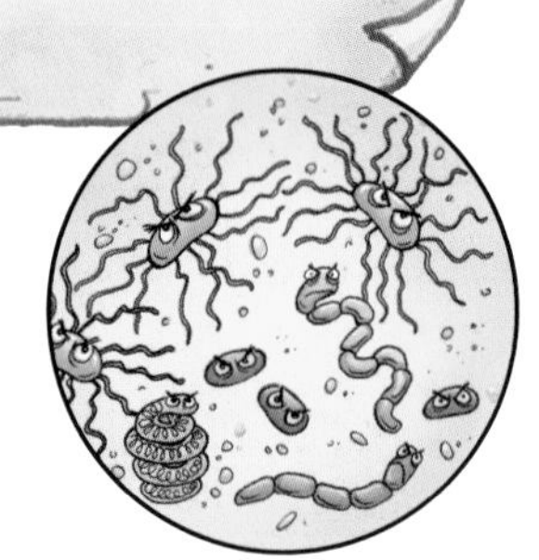

12 August 1348

I am worried. Father Peter the priest has visited most of the houses in the village and says that many people have been unable to work today. He says they feel hot and sweaty, like they have a fever, and that their muscles and bones ache. They sneeze all the time. We pray that it is not the terrible Black Death that everyone is talking about. My friend Anne tells me that her father has the fever.

13 August 1348

Seven more families in the village are ill today. Anne's father has found huge round boils under his armpits and in his groin. He says they are as big as apples! Father Peter has been mixing up some soothing potions and herbs to put on the boils, so perhaps that will help him.

14 August 1348

More and more people are being affected and now my little brother John feels hot and ill all over. Why him O Lord? What harm has he done? Anne's father has now got a rash of black spots all over his body. She says that last night he tried to stick a needle into one of the boils to burst it. It didn't work. Nothing seems to work – even Father Peter's mixture of honey, herbs and vinegar has no effect.

15 August 1348

My brother has got worse overnight. Boils have appeared on his body and his breath smells foul. He has terrible diarrhoea too. Twelve people died yesterday. The church is full of people praying that their loved ones will survive. What sins have we done O Lord? Have we danced too much, or drank too much? God is punishing us all!

16 August 1348

Anne's father is dead. Before he died he was screaming for water. Anne gave him some but his throat was so swollen that he could not swallow it. Perhaps God punished him for drinking ale on Sundays. Anne said that the boils in his armpits burst and smelly black pus dripped on to his deathbed.

The churchyard is now full and men have had to dig one large pit in which to bury all the dead.

17 August 1348

My brother is dying. His boils must be close to bursting now. I have not said anything to mother but now I have the sweating sickness and fever too... I think that soon our village will be very quiet. Will anyone survive? Will it ever end?

WORK

1 Write a sentence to explain the word SYMPTOM, and use a modern day example in your answer. You can use a dictionary to help you.

2 a From the Black Death Diary find at least **five** symptoms of the disease.

b On a simple drawing of a person, explain each symptom of the disease.

3 Read the diary again.

a Identify the different ways people tried to treat the disease.

b Identify the reasons why people thought you caught the Black Death. You will need this information when you are asked to write your own Black Death diary later in this book.

PAUSE FOR THOUGHT

Why do you think that this disease has been called the Black Death?

The Black Death: facts and fiction

- How was the Black Death spread?
- What developments were there in medical knowledge in the Middle Ages?

What we know today...

The Black Death was probably two different types of plague. They attacked at the same time.

1 Bubonic plague

- Came from the germ called pasteurella pestis.
- The germ lived in the blood of black rats and in the gut of their fleas.
- The fleas would bite people and infect them.
- Victims would get a fever and find large lumps (called buboes) in their armpits or groin. They would develop a rash of red and black spots.
- About seven out of ten victims died within a week.

- In medieval England rats were a very common sight, feeding on rubbish that piled up in the streets. Rat fleas bit and fed off the rats as well as biting people. And the rats died of the plague as well.

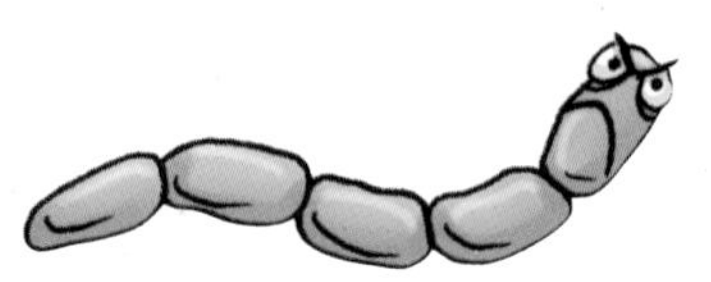

2 Pneumonic plague

- Caught through breathing infected air.
- It attacked the lungs and victims would cough up blood and spray deadly germs as they coughed.
- The victim's breath would begin to smell as their lungs rotted inside them.
- Most victims would be dead within a few days.

... and what they thought in 1348

Medieval doctors didn't really have any idea about how to treat victims of the Black Death. They didn't know how it was caused and they couldn't find a way of curing it. But this didn't stop them from trying.

Crazy causes!

Some people thought the plague was caused by Jews. In Germany 12,000 Jewish men, women and children were burnt to death. Others thought that you could catch it by staring at a victim, wearing pointed shoes or drinking from a poisoned well. However, most people thought the plague was a punishment from God because he was angry with them.

Crazier cures!

People thought they could get rid of the plague by trying one of these weird methods:

- Eating a magic spell that had been written down for them.
- Drinking vinegar or mercury.
- Killing a frog, drying it in the sun, holding it on their boils and watching it suck out the poison.
- Stabbing their boils with a needle.
- Rubbing onions, herbs, figs and a chopped-up snake on the boils.
- Cutting a pigeon in half and rubbing it all over their bodies.

You can see from these ideas that people really didn't know what to do. But they were frightened, and so they were prepared to do just about anything to keep safe.

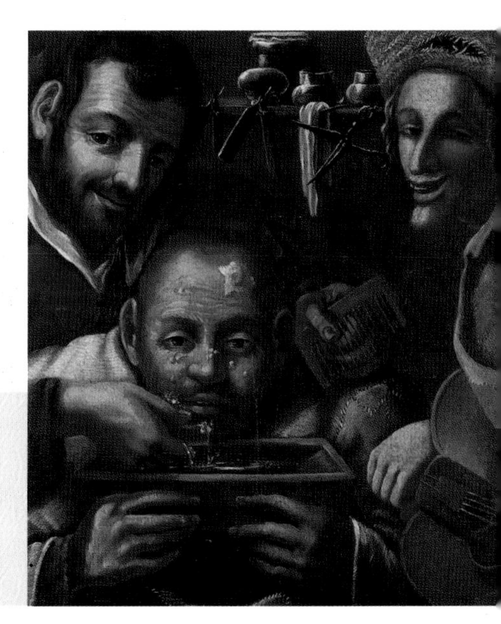

Source A ▸ This painting was made after the time of the Black Death and shows a victim having a boil burst

WORK

1 Copy and complete the following table:

	Bubonic plague	Pneumonic plague
How was it caught?		
What were the symptoms?		
How long did it take to die?		

2 Design a Black Death information leaflet for 1348. Remember that nobody knew what we do about the causes of the plague, so don't include any mention of fleas, germs or rats. Your leaflet should:

- warn people about the causes – add pictures to make the message stronger
- advise people about the cures available
- be eye-catching and informative.

Remember that few people at the time could read. How does this affect the sort of leaflet you will create?

How was the Black Death spread?

AIMS ▸ What were the reasons for the spread of the Black Death in Europe?

The Black Death was first reported in China and India in 1334. Trading ships carried infected rats and people all over Europe without any idea of the deadly disease that was on board. By 1348 the plague had reached Italy, France and Russia. By the time the Black Death had crept across Hungary, Germany and the Netherlands, over 20 million people had died from it.

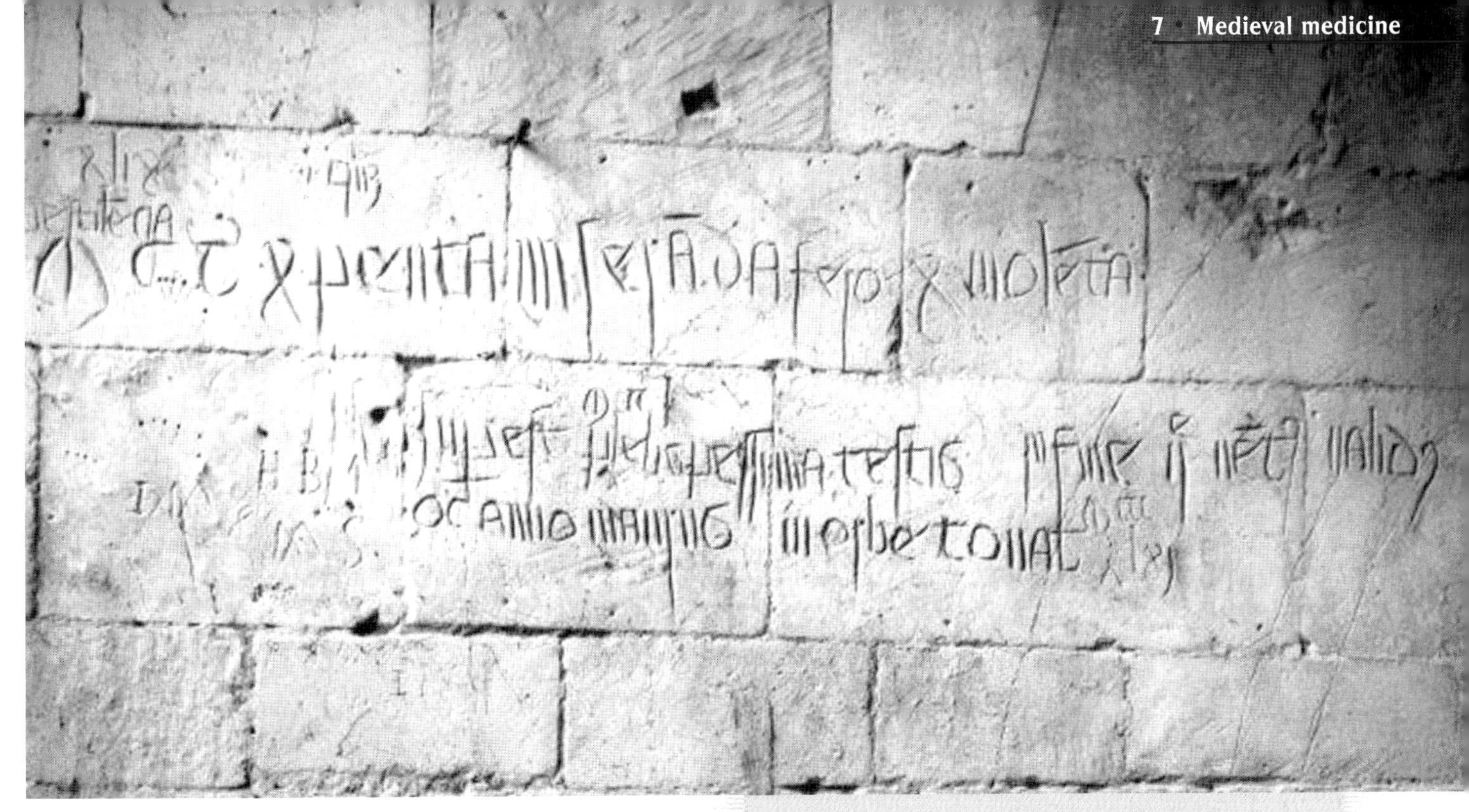

Source C ▲ These words were scratched on a church wall in Ashwell, Hertfordshire. They read "1349 the pestilence. 1350, pitiless, wild, violent, the dregs of the people live to tell the tale."

Source B ▲ An excavation of a medieval plague burial pit at Hereford

Summary

- the Black Death killed at least one third of the population of Europe
- it arrived in Europe in 1347 and terrorised people for about three years
- it was carried by fleas which lived on rats
- the symptoms were horrific and there was no cure

WISE UP WORDS

Symptom Flagellant Plague

WORK

1 How did the Black Death spread across Europe? Think about how the details of how it arrived in England for your answer.

2 What was a 'flagellant'? Why do you think they believed their actions would keep them safe from the disease?

3 Using all the information available to you, write your own Black Death diary. Describe the events as the plague arrives in your town or even your home. Include details of:
   - who is infected – do you know them?
   - symptoms of the disease
   - what you think caused the disease – what stories have you heard?
   - how you are feeling.

Who healed the sick in the Middle Ages?

AIMS ▸ What ideas and practices were there in medieval medicine?

Today we visit the doctor or chemist if we are sick. We trust these people to make us better. They might put us on a course of drugs if they think our illness is serious. If we are cut we might use antiseptics to stop infection. Things were very different in the Middle Ages.

Although there were doctors in the Middle Ages, most of them didn't know much about the real causes of illness. They didn't know that germs were the cause of disease because they had no microscopes with which to see them. There were plenty of places for germs to be found, as you can tell from this description of a house in the Middle Ages.

Source D A description of a medieval house

> The floors are made of clay. They are covered with rushes. Under the rushes is a collection of beer, grease, bones, animal droppings and everything that is nasty.

Medieval doctors believed you could tell what was wrong with someone by examining their urine. He would look at its colour and use a special chart to work out what was wrong. He might even taste it!

Doctors would also use the position of the stars and planets to work out the best time to treat you.

Barber-surgeons

Some doctors believed that 'bad' blood was a cause of illness. This was based on an old Greek and Roman idea that too much blood in a person's body could make them ill. They thought the answer was to make the patient bleed so that their 'bad' blood would disappear and their body would be in balance again. This was called **blood-letting**. People would often visit a **barber-surgeon** to be bled. He was usually cheaper than a doctor and you could have your hair cut at the same time! Barber-surgeons sometimes used **leeches** to suck the blood out of people. The problem was that many barber-surgeons didn't know when to stop bleeding the patients and some died after losing too much blood.

FACT: ▸ Give blood

▸ A barber-surgeon's shop was easy to spot. People would look out for:

- a bowl of fresh blood in the window
- a red-and-white-striped pole: red for the blood and white for the bandages. Some barbers still have poles like these outside their shops today.

Trepanning

A common 'cure' for a headache in the Middle Ages was to ask a doctor to drill a hole in the side of your head. People believed this would let out the evil spirits trapped there. This method was called **trepanning**.

Source F European and Arabic treatments

An Arab doctor was asked to treat a knight with a cut on his leg and a woman with lung disease. He cleaned the knight's leg and put a fresh dressing on it and changed the woman's diet to make her feel better.

A European doctor appeared and laughed at the Arab doctor's ideas. He told the knight that it would be better for him to live with one leg than not to live at all and ordered that the wounded leg should be removed. The knight died with one swing of the axe.

The European doctor then cut open the woman's skull and removed her brain. He rubbed the brain with salt, claiming that this would wash away the devil inside her. The woman, of course, died instantly.

Source E An opinion about doctors from 1380

Doctors possess three qualifications: to be able to lie without being caught out; to pretend to be honest; and to cause death without feeling guilty.

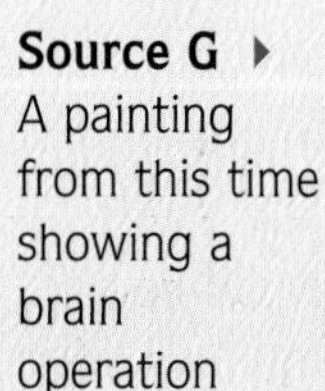

Source G ▸ A painting from this time showing a brain operation

WORK

1 Read **Source D**.
  a Explain why the floor was covered in rushes.
  b How might the floor's contents have been dangerous to a person's health?

2 Make a list of the treatments used by doctors to cure people in the Middle Ages. For each treatment see if you can explain why a doctor might have believed the treatment would work.

3 Read **Source E**.
  a What is this person's opinion of doctors in 1380?
  b Can you think of any reasons why the person might have thought this?

4 Read **Source F**.
  a Who appears to have the best understanding of medicine – the European doctor or the Arabic doctor? Explain your answer.
  b European doctors' understanding of medicine improved greatly after many years of war against the Arabs. Why do you think this might have happened?

5 Study **Source G**.
  a Explain in detail what is happening in the picture.
  b Does this source in any way back up the views in **Source E**? Explain your answer.

Leeches are still used to treat some illnesses today. Find out how leeches are used. What benefits does this treatment give? Are there any examples you can find?

Were any medieval cures for illness effective?

AIMS ▸ What aspects of medieval medicine were helpful?

Most doctors in medieval times didn't really know how to cure disease and illness. But this didn't seem to stop them from trying.

Working in pairs or small groups, see if you can match up the illnesses on the left with the correct cures on the right. (When you have done this, check the answers at the bottom of page 69.) Remember that all these cures were actually used!

Toothache	Hold a live toad next to the skin - it will soon soften the skin.
Warts	Burn some feathers and breathe in the smoke.
Scrofula (a lung disease)	Burn a candle near the tooth. Hold a bowl of cold water underneath. Soon the tooth-eating worms will fall nto the bowl.
Boils	Mix honey, goat dung and herbs together and rub it into the infected area.
Coughing	Touch a king or queen, or a coin that they have used.
Gout	Cut a pigeon in half and rub it into the swollen area.
Fainting	Drink the blood of a black cat. Mix it with some milk.

As you may have worked out, most of these 'cures' had no chance of working. However, doctors weren't the only ones mixing strange potions. **Apothecaries** (medicine makers) used herbs and plants to heal people. As we have come to know more about the healing powers of herbs and plants, we must give the apothecary greater respect.

Foxglove leaves were chewed to help relieve chest pain. Today we know that the leaves contain digitalis which is used to treat heart conditions.

Poppy and henbane seeds were given to relieve pain. Today we know that both these seeds contain natural painkillers (e.g. opium).

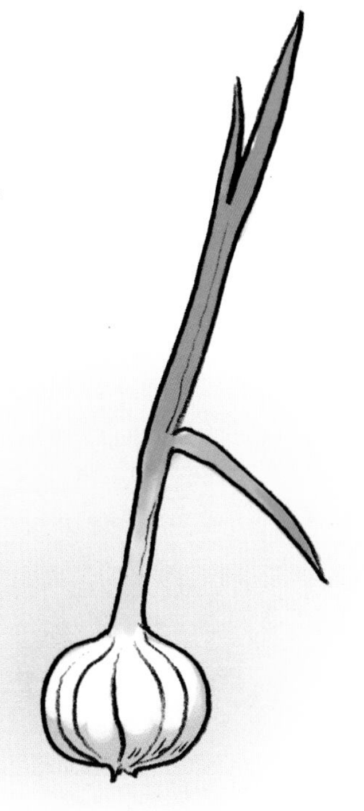

Garlic was given to treat minor infections. Today we know that garlic kills bacteria and helps blood flow.

Willow leaves were used to treat pains such as headaches. You might not have wanted the doctor to drill a hole in your head (trepanning), so you could visit the apothecary. Willow leaves have been found to contain a painkiller very similar to aspirin.

FACT: Stop and think

- Scientists have found over 1000 useful drugs in herbs and plants. There are thousands of plants that haven't yet been studied but which face extinction through pollution and rainforest destruction.

WISE UP WORDS

apothecaries barber-surgeon blood-letting flagellants leeches plague trepanning

WORK

1 Doctors needed a variety of ingredients for their cures. Copy and complete the following table, listing the ingredients needed and adding small pictures to help you to remember.

Illness	Ingredients needed	Picture
Toothache		
Warts		
Boils		
Coughing		
Gout		

2 Why might a patient have been better off visiting an apothecary rather than a doctor in the Middle Ages?

3 Explain why you think doctors today know more about medicine than they did in medieval times.

Summary

- Doctors didn't know much about the causes of disease and illness.
- Blood-letting was one of the most common ways to cure a disease. There were other ideas too, like drilling a hole in someone's head to cure a headache.
- Apothecaries used herbs and plants. They were successful in curing some minor illnesses.

In pairs write a short script for a a role-play activity about a sick person's visit to the doctor in the Middle Ages. One person should act out the role of patient, the other the role of the doctor. Look back at this section for more gruesome ideas!

(Answers to the matching activity: toothache = burn a candle near the tooth; warts = hold a live toad next to the skin; scrofula = touch a king or queen; boils = cut a pigeon in half; coughing = drink the blood of a black cat; gout = mix honey, goat dung and herbs; fainting = burn some feathers.)

Have you been learning?

Task 1

Starting from the bottom right-hand corner, this picture shows an operation in the Middle Ages. Think about the following questions before writing a description of the scene in as much detail as you can.

a What sort of operation is taking place?

b What do you think is wrong with the patient?

c Why is the doctor performing this operation?

d What do you think happened to the patient?

e Write down as many differences as you can see between this operation and a modern-day operation.

Task 2

A homophone is a word that sounds the same as another word but has a different meaning and spelling, for example a sale in the shops and a sail on a ship. The words sound the same but they are not spelt the same.

Copy the sentences below, writing the correct words from the choices in brackets.

a William Rufus was killed whilst shooting (deer/dear) in the (New/Knew) Forest.

b A monk would get up at (too/two) in the (mourning/morning) to (prey/pray).

c (For/Four) (nights/knights) murdered Thomas Becket in Canterbury Cathedral.

d Richard the Lionheart (fort/fought) in the Third Crusade, crossing land and (see/sea) to get to the (Wholly/Holy) Land.

e King Edward I attacked (Whales/Wales) in 1277.

f To avoid catching the Black Death (sum/some) people (ate/eight) magic spells that had (bean/been) written down (for/fore) them.

g If you (caught/court) the Black Death, you (would/wood) usually (die/dye) within one (weak/week).

h In the Middle Ages (sum/some) doctors (would/wood) drill a (hole/whole) in the top of your head to relieve a headache.

Task 3

Medieval kings were often given nicknames. Name the kings who had the following nicknames and then put them in chronological order. When you have done this, explain how each of them got their nickname.

Lackland • The Conqueror • Lionheart • Hammer of the Scots • Rufus • The Confessor

Task 4

Of all the characters you have learned about so far, who is most likely to have said each of the following statements? Write a sentence to explain the choices you have made.

a I have a very smelly job.

b I'm the lowest of the low, everyone is my lord.

c I woke up today at two in the morning to say my prayers.

d You will go to heaven if you die fighting the Saracens.

e I hate the Scots.

f The barons don't support me

Task 5

Here are six groups of words or names. In each group there is an odd one out. When you think you have found it, write a sentence or two to explain why you think it doesn't fit in with any of the others.

1 habit • sword • sandals • tonsure

2 nunnery • monastery • abbey • church

3 Thomas Becket • Richard Britto • Reginald Fitzurse • William de Traci

4 Richard • Phillip • Saladin • Frederick

5 William Wallace • Llywelyn • Edward I • Daffyd

6 boils • bad breath • toothache • diarrhoea

'Let's go and argue with the king!'

- How did the feudal system limit personal freedom?
- What was the background to and early stages of the Peasants' Revolt?

Argue with the king! Sounds ridiculous doesn't it?

From what we know about life in the Middle Ages, the idea of ordinary people arguing with the king may sound ridiculous. This sort of idea was likely to lead to getting your head chopped off. You wouldn't argue with the king – he was as important as God and could do no wrong.

In 1381 a priest called John Ball encouraged peasants in the south of England to go and meet with the king. These people then travelled to London, pulled down houses, set them on fire, murdered some of the king's advisers and met with young King Richard II, who was only 14.

This event is known as the Peasants' Revolt. This section looks at the following questions:

- Why were these men so angry?
- What exactly happened when they got to London?
- Did they really argue with the king?
- How did Richard II treat them?

Why were peasants so fed up?

In May 1381 the king's officials arrived in Fobbing, Essex and tried to collect the new poll tax. Ordinary peasants refused to pay it and attacked the tax collectors. Three collectors were killed but one escaped and rode back to London to tell the king. Other collectors were attacked all over Essex and Kent. The Peasants' Revolt had started.

The peasants' complaints

Follow the leaders

Thousands of peasants met up in Maidstone, just outside London, and chose Wat Tyler, a former soldier, as their leader. First he freed John Ball from Maidstone jail. Ball had been travelling around Kent for months encouraging the peasants to rise up against their lords. The Archbishop of Canterbury had him thrown in jail.

By early June 1381 there were about 60,000 angry peasants armed with sticks, scythes, bows and arrows and any other weapons they could lay their hands on. They wanted to get to London as quickly as possible to talk to the king.

Source A ▲ King Richard II on this throne. As he was so young Richard was helped to rule by advisers, including his uncle – John of Gaunt.

On their journey to London the peasant army continued to riot. They opened jails and let criminals go free, destroyed valuable property and set fire to manor houses. These manor houses often contained many important documents in them like Records of Work Service.

Why do you think the peasants destroyed the Records of Work Service, the documents that laid out the duties each peasant must do for his lord?

Arriving in London, the peasants forced their way through the city gates. Then they broke into Savoy Palace, home of one of the king's hated advisers, his uncle John of Gaunt. All the palace buildings were blown up with gunpowder and his valuables were thrown into the river. One man tried to steal some silver, but Wat Tyler beheaded him, saying that there should be no **looting**.

Rebels continued to arrive in London from all over the country and historians estimate there may have been 100,000 of them.

The king was watching events from the safety of the Tower of London. He knew that his position as king was under threat and London was in chaos. Young Richard sent out a message to the peasants. It said that he would meet everyone in the fields at Mile End, a part of London, the next day.

WORK

1. Explain how each of the following made the peasants so angry in 1381.
   a The Black Death. b Work Service.
   c Poll tax.
2. Match up the names on the left with the correct descriptions on the right.

Wat Tyler	14-year-old king of England
John Ball	The king's uncle and adviser
Richard II	Leader of the Peasants' Revolt
John of Gaunt	Priest who believed all men were equal and should not be forced to work for free

3. If you were Wat Tyler at Mile End with over 100,000 peasants, what would you have done? Would you:
   a burn London to the ground?
   b tell King Richard II your demands and hope he agrees?
   c force the king to agree to all your demands or face death?
   d think up another plan. If so, what's the plan?

   Explain your answer.

The Peasants' Revolt: two days in June

- What were the climax and consequences of the Peasants' Revolt?
- How reliable and useful are the sources available to us from this time?

PAUSE FOR THOUGHT

King Richard II was only 14 years old when the Peasants' Revolt happened. It must have taken great courage to go and meet the angry peasants, but why do you think that he felt he had to go?

On 14 June 1381 Richard was taken by boat along the Thames to meet the peasants' leaders. The crowd were angry and shouted abuse at him. To Richard's surprise, the leaders greeted him by kneeling down and bowing to him. One said, 'We will not have any other king than you.' Wat Tyler explained that the peasants wanted to be allowed to work for the highest wages they could get. Also, they didn't want to have to work for the lords for free, and they certainly didn't want to pay the new increased poll tax.

To everyone's surprise, the king agreed. He said, 'Yes' to everything. He even said he would get his clerks to write free **pardons** for the peasants who had committed crimes during the revolt. The peasants had challenged the king and won... or had they?

Around the time of this meeting a group of rebels broke into the Tower of London and dragged away the Archbishop of Canterbury and the king's treasurer. The angry mob beheaded them both, stuck their heads on spikes and paraded them through the streets of London. Sources from the time say it took eight chops to separate the Archbishop's head from his body. His hat - the mitre - was then nailed to his skull.

15th June 1381

The king met the rebels again at Smithfield in London. With him were about 75 knights and **nobles**. They faced up to 25,000 peasants. Wat Tyler asked the king to divide up all the Church lands among the peasants. He also asked him to make everyone, except the king, equal. Once again, the king agreed.

Tyler then asked for some beer, drank some and spat the rest on to the floor next to the king. This was a terrible insult. Tyler had gone too far and had shown a lack of respect. Read **Sources A** and **B** to find out what happened next.

At that moment the Mayor of London arrived with 12 knights, all well armed, and broke through to speak to the crowd. He said to Tyler, 'Halt! Would you dare to speak like that in front of the king?'

The king began to get angry and told the Mayor, 'Set hands on him.' Tyler said to the Mayor, 'What have I said to annoy you?' 'You lying, stinking, crook,' said the Mayor. 'Would you speak like that in front of the king? By my life, you'll pay dearly for it.'

And the Mayor drew his sword and struck Tyler such a blow to the head that he fell down at the feet of his horse. The knights clustered around him so that he couldn't be seen by the rebels. Then a squire called John Standish drew out his sword and put it to Tyler's belly and so he died.

Seeing their leader killed, the people began to murmur and said, 'Let us go and kill them all.' And they got themselves ready for battle.

Source A ▸ This was written by John Froissant, a French knight, who wasn't present at the Revolt.

Source B ▾ By a monk in 1399. Again, he wasn't present at the time.

> The commons were arrayed in battle formation in great numbers. Tyler dismounted, carrying his dagger. He called for some water and rinsed his mouth in a very rude disgusting fashion in front of the king.
>
> Tyler then made to strike the king's valet [bodyguard] with his dagger. The Mayor of London tried to arrest him, and because of this Wat stabbed the mayor with his dagger in the stomach. But the Mayor, as it pleased God, was wearing armour, and drew his cutlass and gave Wat a deep cut on the neck, and then a great cut on the head.

Source C ▴ Illustration taken from a contemporary manuscript showing the death of Tyler in front of the King.

The rebels were shocked that one of their leaders was dead and as some looked ready to attack him, Richard rode out alone to them and told them: 'Sirs, what is the matter? You shall have no leader except me. I am your king. Be peaceful.'

Almost immediately, the situation was calmed and shortly afterwards the peasants began to go home.

But King Richard didn't keep his promises. His army hunted down many of the ringleaders and killed them. John Ball, like Wat Tyler, had his head cut off and put on a spike on London Bridge. It looked as if the revolt had been a total failure.

However, over the next 50 years, the peasants did receive most of the things they had asked for, but on the king's terms. To begin with, the poll tax was scrapped. The king eventually stopped trying to control the peasants' wages and they could work for the best money they could get. Also, more and more peasants received freedom from their lords. More importantly, the Peasants' Revolt had showed the king that ordinary people could be powerful if they joined together.

WISE UP WORDS

looting nobles pardons poll tax revolt

WORK

1. On 14 June the king agreed to the peasants' demands, but what happened that day which changed his mind?
2. Read **Sources A** and **B**.
   a. What differences are there between the two sources? Give examples.
   b. Why might these two sources give such different versions of events?
   c. Do you think the writer of **Source B** supported Tyler or not? Make a list of the words or phrases which show whether he does or does not support him.
3. Design a newspaper front page for the events of the Peasants' Revolt. Your paper supports the king, so make sure you include **bias** in your descriptive writing. Add quotes, illustrations – maybe an advert of something people might have bought in the Middle Ages.

Summary

- The Peasants' Revolt had several causes, including the effects of the Black Death and the new poll tax.
- Led by Wat Tyler and John Ball, the peasants marched to London with a list of demands.
- The king agreed to the demands but then Tyler and Ball were killed. The king had changed his mind.
- Over the next 50 years, however, most of the peasants' demands were met.

How were people punished in the Middle Ages?

- What was the importance of the trial by ordeal system of justice?
- What role did God play in the process?

There was no police force in England in the Middle Ages. If you saw someone committing a crime you would shout as loudly as you could and everyone within earshot would have to help hunt for the criminal. This was called 'raising the **hue and cry**'. If the villagers didn't help, they would be fined.

When caught for a small crime the criminal would be taken to the local lord's manor house. The lord would then decide on the punishment, which would usually be a fine.

Today's fines ...

More serious crimes were dealt with by the king's court. If the case was unclear, the king, or one of his **sheriffs**, would probably order a trial by **ordeal**.

FACT: God as the judge

- Everyone believed in God in medieval times. They believed that God helped good people and punished bad people. Trial by ordeal was a way of allowing God to decide on someone's guilt.

Ordeal by fire

Step 1 The accused carries a red-hot iron bar for three steps, or takes a stone from the bottom of a pot of boiling water.

Step 2 The prisoner's hand is bandaged, and he returns to court three days later.

Verdict If the wound has healed, God must think the prisoner is worth helping and so he must be innocent. If the wound is infected, God must think the prisoner is not worth healing and so he must be guilty. He must be punished by being put to death.

Ordeal by water

Step 1 The accused is tied up.

Step 2 He is thrown into a lake or river.

Verdict Water is pure, just like God. If the prisoner floats, the water doesn't want him, nor does God. If God has rejected him, he must be guilty. He was put to death. If the prisoner sinks and drowns, God must want him in heaven. He must be innocent.

Ordeal by combat

This was a trial for rich people. The accuser would fight the accused. It was possible to get someone called a champion to fight for you. For some people this was their job, earning huge amounts of money fighting on behalf of different lords.

Step 1 Both sides should select their weapons. These would be made from wood and bone.

Step 2 The accuser and the accused (or their champions) must fight for as long as possible, starting at sunrise.

Verdict People believed God would give the winner extra strength. The first person to surrender was thought to be guilty and therefore must be punished by being put to death.

FACT: God help me!

- If you were 'on the run', there was one lawful way to escape punishment – hide in a church and claim **sanctuary**. Claiming sanctuary meant that you would be safe in the church for 40 days. In that time you could own up or escape. If you owned up you would be forced to leave England for ever (or you could pretend to leave and hide in the woods as an outlaw).

Source A An account of trial by combat (Medieval Realms, Colin Shephard).

> They were dressed in white leather and had wooden staves... they had neither meat nor drink... if they needed anything to drink they had to drink their own piss... they bit with their teeth so that the leather and their flesh was torn in many places. James grabbed Thomas by the nose with his teeth and put his thumb in his eye. Thomas called for mercy and the judge stopped the fight. Thomas admitted he had wrongly accused James and was hanged.

WORK

1. a If you raised the 'hue and cry', what would you be doing?

   b Why was it important to make sure everybody took notice of the 'hue and cry'?

2. Copy and complete the following paragraph using the missing words below.

   Small crimes were dealt with in the ____________ manor house. The criminal would usually be punished with a ____________. The ____________ court would deal with the more serious crimes. If the king, or one of his ____________, couldn't decide what had happened, they might order trial by ____________. This means they would allow ____________ to decide if a person was guilty or not.

   king's • sheriffs • lord's • ordeal • God • fine

3. Why did many people in the Middle Ages believe ordeal by water or fire was the best way to find out if a person was guilty or not?

4. Why do you think trial by combat was only used by rich people?

5. Looking at the trial process, do you think it was possible to get justice in the Middle Ages? What are your reasons for your answer?

Crimewatch!

- What were typical medieval crimes and punishments?
- How important were the changes to the law made by King Henry II?

In the Middle Ages the king made the laws and wanted everyone to obey them. When people didn't follow the rules and broke the law, the local lord or the king said they must be punished. Most punishments took place in public as a warning to others. Often the punishment fitted the crime.

The thief

Name: Elizabeth Hayes
Place: Southwark, 1195
Crime: Broke into the house of Francis Willmore and stole two linen sheets.
Punishment: To be taken to the pillory and whipped for 16 lashes.

The liar

Name: Anthony Fowlkes
Place: London, 1452
Crime: Told lies to certain citizens about what he had seen.
Punishment: To be put into the pillory, with one ear nailed to it. (After two days it was time to set Fowlkes free, but his bloody ear had stuck to the pillory, so they had to cut it off!)

The conman

Name: John Bird
Place: London, 1327
Crime: When neighbours came to bake their bread in his oven, Bird first placed it on a table. A servant, sitting in secret underneath the table, cut a hole in the bottom of the loaf and stole some of the dough.
Punishment: To be dragged through the streets on a hurdle with some rotten loaves tied around his neck. Then to be put in the stocks for two days.

The coin-clipper

Name: William Baynard
Place: Winchester, 1124
Crime: Clipped off and kept small amounts of silver from the edges of King Henry's coins. The silver should have gone into coins used to pay soldiers fighting in France.
Punishment: To have his right hand tied to a block of wood, an axe placed over his wrist and hit with a hammer until his hand is cut off. Then the same to happen to his genitals.

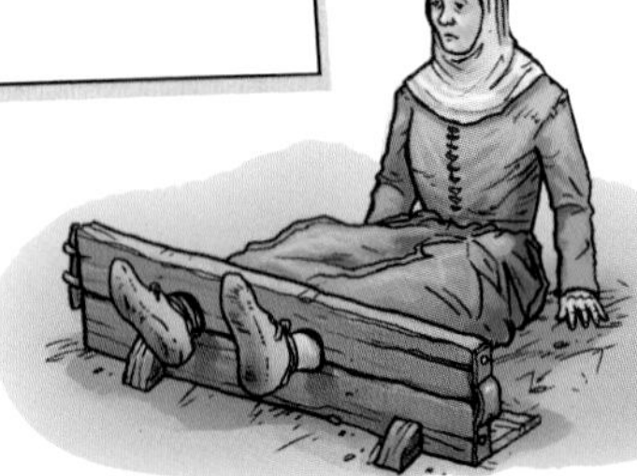

The lunatic

Name: Andrew Friday
Place: Raveningham, 1307
Crime: Stole a horse belonging to John of Hales worth 20 shillings and sold it to Peter Monk of Norwich for 8 shillings.
Punishment: The jury said Friday was insane before and after the theft. Fifteen days before the theft he had cut down all the trees near his home and then replanted them. After his arrest he was put in prison, where he ate his clothes. Then he tore at the shoes of other prisoners with his teeth. It was decided that he was insane, so he was freed.

The rebel

Name: Earl Waltheof
Place: Winchester, 1077
Crime: Treason (a crime against the king). Led an armed rebellion against King William I.
Punishment: To be beheaded. Waltheof cried so much he couldn't finish saying the lord's prayer. The executioner lost his temper and cut off his head anyway.

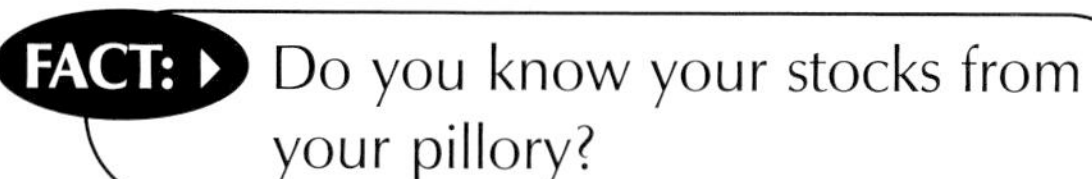

Do you know your stocks from your pillory?

- **Stocks** These were used for punishing minor crimes like poaching or letting your animals wander on to someone else's land. A prisoner's feet were locked into the stocks for a certain period of time. Passers-by could shout abuse and throw rotten vegetables.
- **Pillory** Again, this was used for minor crimes. His ears might be nailed to the wood too. Often a large stone was hung around the prisoner's neck. Naughty children might be taken to a finger pillory which trapped just the fingertips.

Trial by jury

King Henry II made some important changes to the law system in England. He decided that trial by ordeal wasn't really suitable for serious crimes such as robbery or murder. He sent judges around the country to set up courts known as the Court of the King's Bench. These judges would ask 12 local men to tell them all about the prisoner. The judges would then decide whether the prisoner was guilty or not. In later years, a jury of 12 people would decide a person's guilt. This system of trial by jury is still in use today.

WISE UP WORDS

hue and cry jury ordeal pillory sanctuary sheriffs stocks treason

WORK

1 What is meant by the term 'the punishment fitted the crime'? Give examples to go with your explanation.

2 a What was the difference between the stocks and the pillory?

b Which one do you think a criminal would fear the most? Give reasons for your answer.

3 Imagine the year is 1150 and a criminal is on the loose in your town. Design a 'wanted' poster to make people aware of his crimes. You should include:

- his/her name, age and description
- details of their crime. What have they done? Should the other townspeople be careful? Are they dangerous?
- notes about what any punishment is likely to be. Remember that the punishment usually fitted the crime.

Summary

- By today's standards trials by fire, water or combat were not very fair. Innocent people must have been found guilty.
- Punishments usually fitted the crime and were a lot harsher than today.
- King Henry II made important changes to the law system and some of the ideas are still used today.

What was life like in a medieval village?

- How did ordinary people live in the past?

England was full of small villages in the Middle Ages. Most people lived in these villages and farmed the land. Most of the land was owned by the lord of the manor, who was usually a knight. The lord let the peasants live on the land in return for them obeying him and working for him three days a week.

The villeins (peasant villagers) worked very hard. They grew wheat for bread, barley for beer, oats, rye (to feed the animals), vegetables and fruit. They kept sheep, pigs, goats, chickens and cows. If there was a bad harvest or their animals died of disease or cold, the villeins could starve to death.

Some of the people travelled to other villages because they had special jobs such as being a carpenter or a blacksmith, but most of them worked their entire lives in the same small village where they were born. Some peasants never even travelled to the next town, because they needed their lord's permission to do so!

How does this villager spend his day?

He gets up when it's light enough to see and works all day. In the spring he ploughs the land and plants seeds. In the summer he harvests the hay, weeds the corn and scares the birds. In the autumn he harvests the corn and kills and salts some animals for winter. In winter he would clear any wasteland, repair his hut and tools and, most importantly, try and keep warm.

What do they eat?

- Breakfast – 6am. Bread and ale to drink (water wasn't safe).
- Lunch – 10am. Bread, perhaps an egg, a piece of or cheese. Ale to drink.
- Supper – 4pm. Bread and pottage (a thick vegetable soup). Ale to drink.

What about his wife?

She works as hard as he does. She cooks, cleans and looks after the children. She fetches water, makes and mends clothes and helps out in the fields when she is needed.

Where do they live?

In a one-room hut. The frame is made from wood and the walls are made from **wattle** (sticks woven together) and **daub** (mud, dung and straw). There are no windows and the floor is made of mud mixed with straw and ox blood to make it hard. There is a hole in the roof to let out the smoke from the fire inside. The animals lived in the hut too... what a smell!

Couldn't the villeins just run away?

No, they weren't allowed – the lord owned them. If they did escape, they would go to court and be punished. Some villeins dreamed of earning enough money to buy their freedom and become freemen.

PAUSE FOR THOUGHT

How many people do you usually see in one day? One hundred, three hundred, perhaps even more? You probably see more people in one day than a villager in the Middle Ages saw in their whole life.

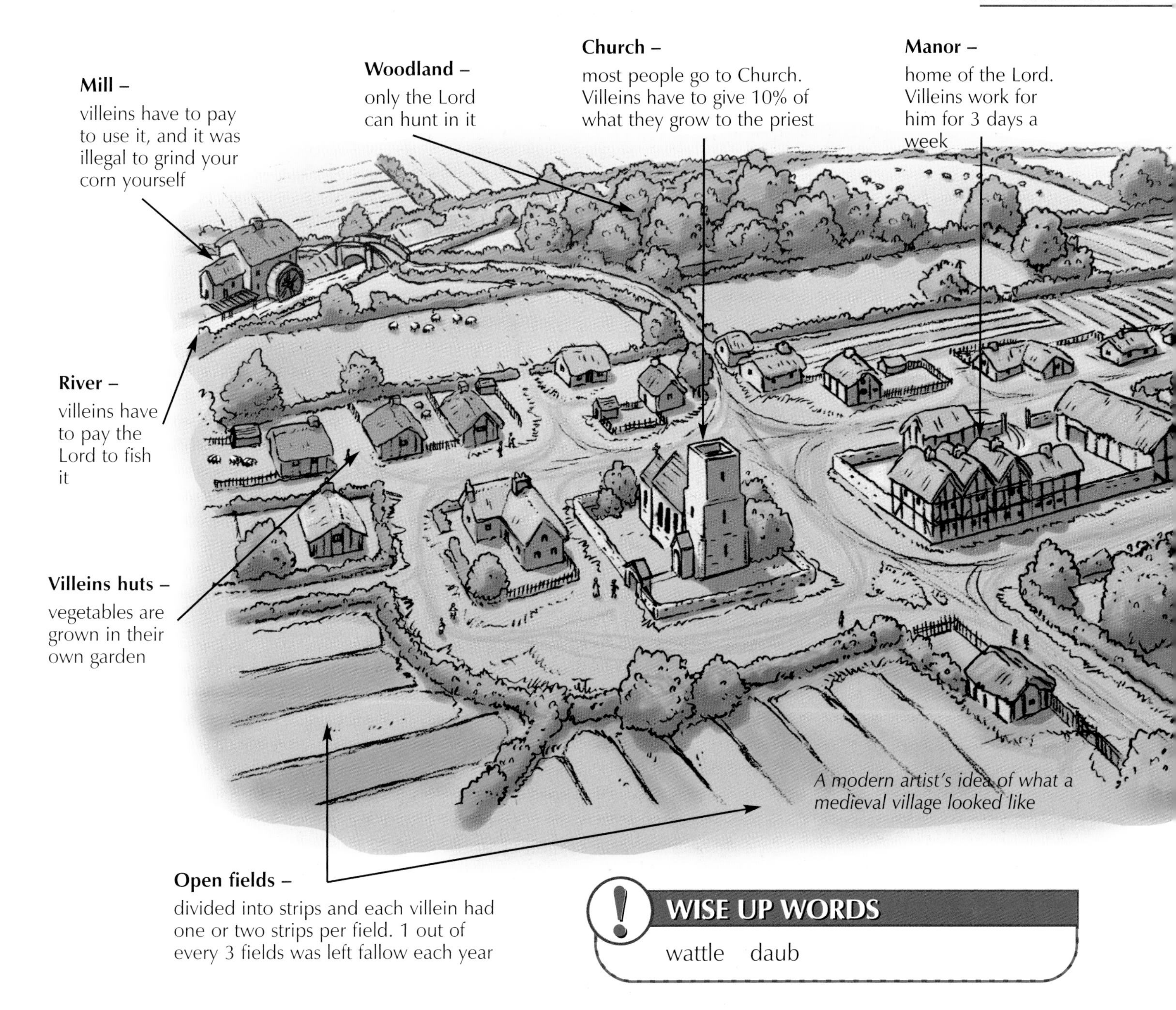

A modern artist's idea of what a medieval village looked like

WISE UP WORDS

wattle daub

WORK

1. a Make a list of the kinds of food people ate in the Middle Ages.
   b Write down three ways in which these foods are different to your meals today.
   c In your opinion, who has the healthier diet? Give reasons for your answer.
2. Why did most people spend all of their lives in the same village?
3. Imagine you are a villein in a medieval village. Write a description of a day in your life. Try to include as much detail as possible. Here are some ideas to think about.
   - What time of year is it?
   - How does your working day change throughout the year?
   - What places will you work in or visit?
   - What sort of people will you meet?
   - Is there a particular type of food you enjoy?
   - At what times do you eat?

What was life like in a medieval town?

- Why did towns grow in medieval times?
- What were the features of a medieval town?

When William conquered England in 1066 there were only about ten towns in the whole country. London was the largest with about 10,000 people, followed by Winchester and Norwich with about 2,500 people each. More people lived in small villages in the countryside, with no more than 50 people living in them.

After 1066 towns began to grow. Sometimes they grew around crossroads or a bridge where people came to buy and sell goods. Others grew near a castle or monastery. The local lord still owned these places but, if the town continued to grow and the townspeople made lots of money, they might join together and buy their land and their freedom. This

freedom – written down on a special piece of paper and known as a charter – gave the townspeople a chance to run the town themselves.

By 1400 about 300 towns had received their charter of freedom. By this time London's population had grown to over 40,000.

Sign language

Most people couldn't read, so special signs hung outside shops to show people what was on sale inside. Can you tell what some of these shops are selling?

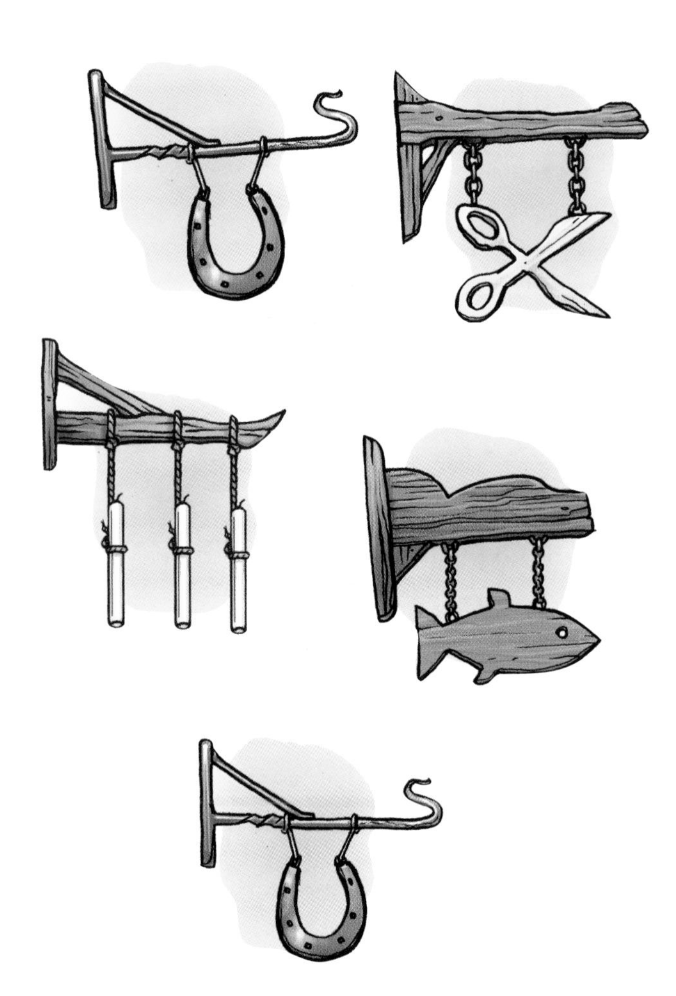

Even today some streets are still named after the traders that used to work there long ago. Does your town have a Fish Street, Smith Street, Cutler's Row, Salt Lane, Butcher's Row or Saddlergate?

FACT: Guilds

- A **guild** was a group or club made up of traders and craftsmen. The guild made rules for its members to follow. They set prices, organised training and made sure that goods were well made. There were guilds for weavers, shoemakers, butchers, bakers, tailors and many more. Some of these guilds can still be found today.
Perhaps you can think of some organisations that monitor the quality and the price of the things we buy or the jobs we have done in our homes?

WORK

1 Explain the meaning of the following words:
population • charter • guild

2 Find the correct numbers to answer the questions below.
  a How many towns were there in England by 1066?
  b How many people were living in London by 1066?
  c What was the approximate number of people living in a small village in 1066?
  d How many towns had received their charter of freedom by 1400?
  e How many people were living in London by 1400?
  Can you add all the numbers for a) to e) correctly? If so you should have the answer 50, 360

3 Why do you think so many towns grew near a castle or monastery?

4 Why was a market important in the lives of people in the Middle Ages?

5 Imagine you have just spent an hour in the town in the picture. Write a short description of the time you spent there. Include details about the sights, sounds and smells of the place. Use as many descriptive words as you can.

Summary

- For a long time most people lived and worked in villages, and many never lived anywhere else.
- Towns started to grow around busy markets, bridges, crossroads, castles and monasteries.

Could you have fun in the Middle Ages?

- What are the origins of the word 'holiday'?
- How did poor and rich people enjoy their leisure time?
- What are the similarities and differences between sports today and sports in the Middle Ages?

In medieval times ordinary people didn't have holidays. Instead, there were a number of church festivals and feast days throughout the year. On these days, after going to a church service, peasants would be free to enjoy themselves. Our word 'holiday' comes from the word 'holy day'.

Peasants had to make their own fun using whatever they had to hand. Some of the amusements were so popular that they are still used by us today.

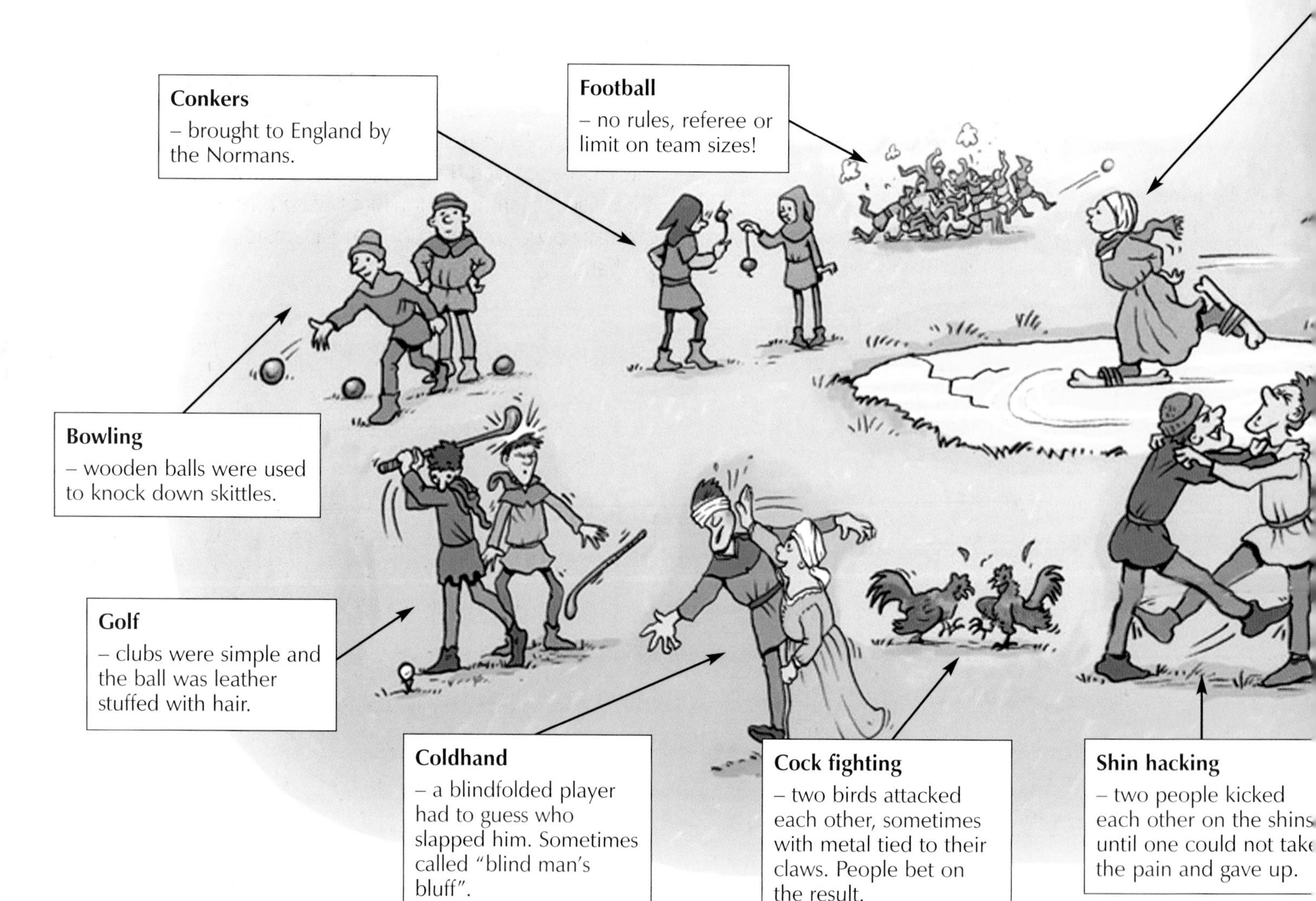

Ordinary people enjoyin

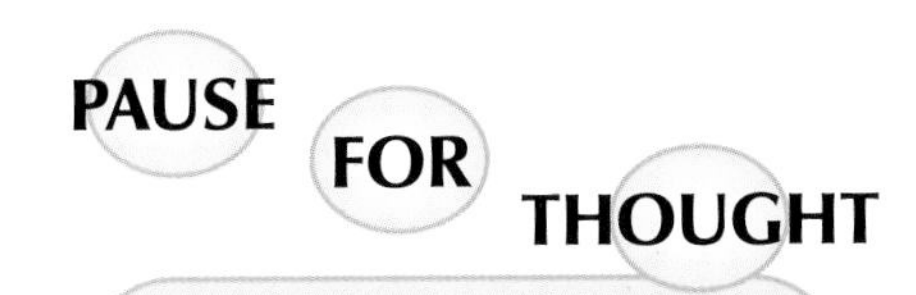

Which of the amusements in the illustration are still enjoyed today? Have any been changed at all? Have some stayed the same throughout the years?

Ice skating
– people strapped sharpened animal bones to their shoes.

Stoolball
– a lady sat on a stool and men threw a ball at her. She tried to dodge, or hit, the ball.

Bear baiting
– a bear was chained to a post while dogs attacked it. People bet on the result.

Wrestling
– all sorts of fighting games were popular.

heir 'Holy Days'

The rich

A rich noble may have gone to a **tournament**. This was a chance to take part in mock battles on horses and challenge another man to joust. He might go hunting in his forest, or stay in his manor house or castle to enjoy feasting or dancing. A group of acrobats or jugglers might entertain his guests. If the party got bored with the entertainers, they might play chess, draughts, cards, or throw dice.

In the Middle Ages a popular game for rich men was real tennis. Two players had to hit a wooden ball over a rope with a racquet. Sometimes the ball was hit so hard that players were killed by a ball hitting them on the head!

Do it yourself...

Whether you were rich or poor, you had to make your own fun in the Middle Ages. There were no cinemas or theatres to visit. You couldn't even go to an organised, professional sports match. But people must have enjoyed their spare time because they didn't get much of it. Holy days were rare, so ordinary people made sure that they made the most of them.

WORK

1 Explain where the modern word 'holiday' comes from.

2 a Look closely at the illustration showing ordinary people enjoying their holy days. Make two lists, one headed 'Things we no longer enjoy today' and the other headed 'Things we still enjoy today'.

b Choose one example from your list of things we no longer enjoy today. Explain why you think this pastime is no longer practised.

c Choose one example from your list of things we still enjoy today. Explain in what ways, if any, it has changed since medieval times.

3 Design a poster to advertise a medieval holy day in your town. Make sure you include the name of the holy day, a programme of events and fun activities taking place. Add some illustrations. Remember all holy days began with a church service.

Has football changed much since the Middle Ages?

- How have people been enjoying football for centuries?
- What are the similarities and differences between football past and present?

About 1,000 years ago a small army from Denmark landed on the English coast and tried to steal as much as they could before sailing away again. However, their leader, a Danish prince, was captured and the angry English chopped off his head. The Englishmen split into two teams and kicked the severed head amongst each other. Football was born.

This game soon became known as 'mob football' when all the men from one village or town played another. It was very violent. There could be as many as 500 players, with few rules, no referee and the goals many miles apart. In Workington an old rulebook said that players could use any method to get the ball to its target except murder. The ball was a pig's bladder, stuffed with dried peas or sawdust.

Game of football

CHESTER
v
CHRISTLETON

Date: Shrove Tuesday, 1175
Time: All day
Rule no.1: There are no rules!

Players are allowed to punch, kick, wrestle, use clubs and sticks. The ball can be carried, kicked, passed and thrown – whatever it takes to get it in the goal.

Source A ▸ A more modern view of football in the Middle Ages. A monk once described it as 'a devilish pastime. More a bloody murdering practice than a sport.'

Source B ▸ A modern game of football. Can you spot any differences with mob football of the past?

Football was regularly banned. In 1314 the Mayor of London banned it because it caused 'great uproar and violence in the city'. The ban was ignored. In 1331 King Edward III became the first king to ban football. He said that people were playing it so much that they were forgetting to practise their archery skills. The king was worried that if a foreign army invaded England the men would have forgotten how to use their bows and arrows properly. The ban didn't last long.

Richard II, Henry IV and Henry V also tried to ban football, but people were so determined to play that they carried on regardless. In Scotland, King James I once famously ruled that 'na man play at the fute-ball' but the Scots loved the game so much that they were playing the game in Edinburgh the next week!

FACT: ▸ Women's football

- In the late 1400s, in the town of Inveresk in Scotland, a group of married and unmarried women started to play each other every few months. The married women regularly won. Women's football is not as new as some people would like to think.

FACT: ▸ A dangerous game

- In 1321 the Pope issued a special letter of forgiveness to a player who had accidentally killed an opponent. A few days later a Londoner wrote that players used to 'retire home as from battle, with bloody heads, bones broken and out of joint and bruises that will shorten their days'. By 1450 players in some towns introduced a new rule to try to reduce the number of accidents: the ball could only be kicked, not carried or thrown.

HUNGRY FOR MORE? *'Mob football' is still played in some parts of Britain today. Try to find out a bit more about this sport. Where is it played? Who plays it? How often? What are the rules? How do the players score?*

WORK

1 Write these statements in the correct chronological order.
- Women's football played regularly in Inveresk, Scotland.
- A new rule was introduced in some towns saying the ball could only be kicked, not picked up.
- King Edward III was the first king to ban football.
- A Danish prince had his head used a ball.
- The Pope issued a special letter to forgive a player who killed an opponent.

2 Which of the above events do you think had the biggest effect on the game of football? Explain your answer.

3 a Make a list of all the differences you can find between football in the Middle Ages and football today.

b What do you think the biggest difference is? Explain your answer.

4 a Why do you think so many kings tried to ban football?

b Why do you think the bans weren't very successful?

Summary

- Many of our modern day sports were played in the Middle Ages.
- Many sports were violent and the rules varied from place to place.
- Blood sports of bear baiting and cock fighting are now banned in Britain.

Enough of history: What about *her* story?

- What was everyday life like for medieval women?
- Why do historians know less about the role of women in medieval England?

What about women in medieval times? What role did they play in shaping our history? What role did they play in everyday life on the farms and why is it so difficult to find out anything about them?

Ordinary women's lives were tough. Most peasant girls learned all they needed to know from their mothers. They learned to cook, sew and care for children and animals. Most girls were married by the time they were 14 years of age. There were no teenage years; you were either a child or an adult.

Unlike men, women had very few rights. In fact, their husbands practically owned them.

In the Middle Ages woman weren't as important as men. They were seen by many as **inferior**. If a husband felt his wife was nagging him too much or gossiping, he could, quite legally, order her to be put in a **scold's bridle**.

Source C ▸ In 1316 Anne Stafford embarrassed her husband in public by calling him a 'foul villain'. She was put in a scold's bridle for four days.

Women cannot:

- marry without her parents' permission
- own property, clothes or jewellery – it belongs to her husband
- divorce husband, even if he beats her
- train to be a doctor, lawyer, priest or judge
- go to the shops, inns or travel on her own
- wear tight or revealing clothes
- speak rudely

Look carefully at the following sources. Decide for yourself what role ordinary women played in everyday life.

Source D ▲ The women's job was to look after the baby and make sure food was prepared.

Source E ▼ From a medieval book

> She hears her child scream, sees the cat eating the bacon and the dog eating the leather. Her bread is burning on the fire, her calf is drinking the milk, the pot is running into the fire and her husband is shouting.

Source F ▶ Women were responsible for milking the cows

Source G ▼ From a medieval book

> They earn by spinning. They spend on rent, milk or porridge to stop the crying of the children. They themselves suffer much hunger. They wake at midnight to rock the cradle, mend clothes and wash them.

Source H ▶ A picture of a hardworking woman drawn in about 1250

Rich women

Like today, women usually lived longer than men. If a wife died after her husband, she would **inherit** his property. Finally then would she be able to make her own decisions.

Out of every 100 people, about two were rich. They would usually live in a castle or manor house with their husband and family. The women wouldn't have chosen her husband – her family would have done that for her. The husband would receive a **dowry** – a payment from the woman's family when he married her.

The wife would learn to read, sew, play an instrument and sing. Like the peasant women, though, she would still have no rights and her husband would make all the decisions.

Do you think it was a good idea for parents to choose a husband for their daughter? Give a reason for your answer.

WISE UP WORDS

daub dowry guild inferior inherit scold's bridle tournament wattle

WORK

1 Copy and complete the following paragraph using the missing words below.

A ________________ woman's life was tough. Most girls were married at the age of ________________. Women had very few rights in the Middle Ages. For example, it was illegal for a wife to own her own ________________, clothes or jewellery. Women were seen by many as being ________________, and nagging wives could be forced to wear a ________________ bridle.

property • scold's • peasant • inferior • 14

2 Study **Sources C** to **H**.

a Make a list of all the different jobs a peasant woman was expected to do. Then make another list of all the different jobs that are done in your own home. Next to each job write the name of the person that does that job.

b Write a paragraph comparing your lists. Are the jobs divided up more evenly today? Give reasons for your answer.

3 Read 'Women cannot:'

a What evidence can you find that women were not treated as equals with men?

b Can you explain why, compared to men, we know less about women from the Middle Ages?

Knight life

- What was the importance and role of the knight in medieval society?
- How do aspects of medieval history still have relevance today?

- Have you ever kicked a football out of play because an opponent is injured?
- Have you ever given up your seat on a bus for an elderly person or a pregnant woman?

If the answer to either of these questions is 'Yes', you are trying to follow a set of unwritten rules called **chivalry**. You don't have to do any of these things, but sometimes you feel better if you do.

Many sports contain some elements of chivalry. For example, when playing golf, there are no rules to stop you making a noise when your opponent is taking a shot. However, players are quiet when their opponent is playing because they don't want to be seen as unsporting. This idea of behaving in the correct manner has been passed down to us from the Middle Ages. It all started with the best warriors in Europe – the knights.

William the Conqueror brought the first knights to England in 1066 to fight King Harold. As a reward for fighting, King William gave them land. In return they promised to spend 40 days a year fighting for him. This was called paying **homage**. As you will see, a knight's life was a busy one.

Code of chivalry

- Be brave at all times.
- Spend money carefully.
- Choose friends wisely.
- Always be prepared for battle.
- Seek revenge if you are insulted.
- Treat your lady well. Fight for her, do brave things for her, write poems for her and be prepared to die for her.
- Never break a promise.
- Help people who cannot defend themselves.

Knight school

A knight's training would start at seven years of age. He would probably come from a rich, noble family. As a boy he would be sent to a knight's home to serve him for about five years. The **page**, as the boy would be known, would clean dishes, serve meals and wash clothes. He might learn to read and write.

At about 14 years old the page would become a **squire**. He would learn about chivalry, weapons, fighting, armour and horses. If the squire worked hard for five years, he would be ready to go through to his knighting ceremony. The squire would be ordered to spend a night in a local church praying. In the morning a priest would bless a sword and instruct the older knight to **dub** the young squire. The squire would kneel down before his master and allow the knight to touch (or dub) his shoulders with the sword. A knight was born.

Tournaments or mêlées

To amuse themselves knights organised tournaments or **mêlées** to practise their skills. Knights would meet in a huge field, divide into two teams and spend the next few hours fighting each other. They didn't want to kill each other so they used blunt weapons, but many knights were still killed by accident.

Jousting

A **joust** was a contest between two knights on horseback. They would ride at each other ten times and one would try to hit the other with a three-metre long lance. Three points were awarded if he knocked his opponent off his horse, two points if he hit his helmet and one point if he hit any other part of his body. A point would be lost if he hit the horse.

Some knights made a living out of winning jousting competitions but the prizes were rather unusual. Often the prize was a golden cup or a silver plate, but in 1216 in London the prize was a huge brown bear!

Armour

A suit of armour could cost up to £75,000 in today's money. Most suits looked the same, so knights painted their own family's coat of arms on their shield to make sure they could be recognised in battle. Some knights even attached something on top of their helmet. Sir William Sidney attached a large silver porcupine to the top of his!

Knights in battle

If a knight was captured in battle he would rarely get killed because he was valuable and his family would pay a ransom to get him freed. Captured knights were treated with great respect – another example of chivalry. When Edward, the Black Prince, defeated King John of France in 1356, he served food to the captured king at the victory feast. The Black Prince said it was a great honour to serve such a brilliant warrior.

WORK

1. Explain the words *chivalry, page, squire, dub, jousting* and *ransom*.
2. Make a list of five things that you do today that could belong to a modern code of chivalry.
3. Why did tournaments, mêlées and jousting play such an important part in a knight's life?
4. Knights would often have their family's coat of arms on their shield. In what situation do you think this might be important?
5. In pairs or small groups, write a code of chivalry for your classroom or school. Think it through carefully. You might put it on display and try to follow it.

Whose side are you on?

- How did knights identify each other in battle?
- What is heraldry?

Once a knight put on his armour, he looked the same as any other knight. To avoid being killed by his own men, the knight decorated his shield with special colours and patterns called coats of arms. Sometimes the knight would also wear a tunic in the same colours as his shield.

These coats of arms had to be easily recognised – you had to know instantly who was coming towards you, so you knew which side he was on. As the years went by, the patterns became very complicated and there were complex rules, called **heraldry**, for their creation.

Rules of Heraldry

1. Patterns can be displayed on a shield, clothing or a standard
2. Design of the coat of arms could use up to five colours – purple, blue, red, black and green – and two 'metals' – gold or silver
3. Shields could be divided into basic patterns, like these basic shapes

Correct ✔

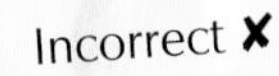

4. If the shield was divided by a pattern, you couldn't put a metal on a metal, or a colour on a colour
5. Coats of arms often had a 'charge' – an image that represented something about him or his family

Symbol or 'Charge'	Meaning
Anchor	Hope
Bear	Strength or protection
Boar	Bravery
Bull	Generosity
Camel	Patience
Castle	Safety
Dolphin	Speed and love
Dragon	Valour or protection
Eagle	Strength, alertness
Goose	Resourcefulness
Griffin	Strength, courage
Hand	Faithfulness, good judgement
Hawk	Determination
Heart	Affection
Holly	Truth
Horse	Ready for anything
Horseshoe	Good luck
Lion	Courage
Otter	Lives life to the full
Peacock	Beauty, power and knowledge
Rainbow	Good times after bad
Red rose	Beauty
Snake	Wisdom
Swan	A good learner
Sword	A good judge
Unicorn	Very, very brave
White rose	Faith and love

The family rules

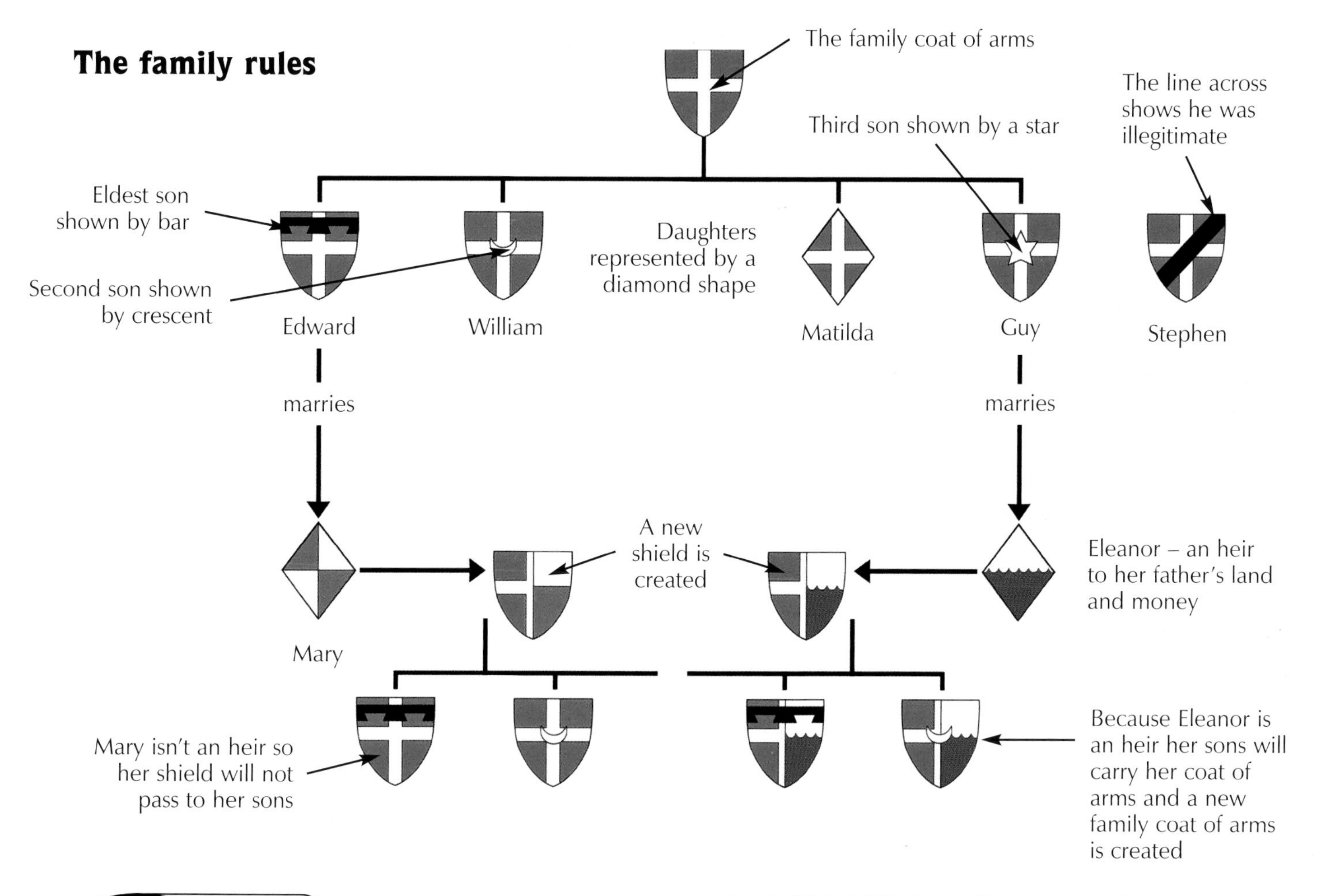

FACT: A herald

- A herald was a man who knew all about this complicated system of heraldry. He worked for the king or a baron. During a battle he would carry messages between the two armies and afterwards he had the horrible job of working out who the dead or dying were by looking at their coats of arms.

HUNGRY FOR MORE?

Carry out your own research into one of these famous knights. Write a short fact file about him, remembering to include a picture of his coat of arms.

- ***Edward, the Black Prince*** *(1330–1376) Son of Edward III.*
- ***Ulrich of Liechtenstein*** *(c.1200s) Lady lover.*
- ***El Cid*** *(1040–1099) The Spanish champion.*
- ***John of Bohemia*** *(1296–1346) A blind knight.*

WORK

1 Copy this paragraph, choosing the correct words from the choice in brackets.

A knight would decorate his shield with a special pattern called a coat of (arms/legs). He would have to follow a complicated set of rules called (astrology/heraldry) when he created this pattern. Sometimes a knight would put a (charge/badge) on the pattern to represent something about him or his family. As well as his shield, the pattern could be displayed on a (tunic/basic) and a (tunic/standard).

2 Choose five charges that best describe you and your family. Draw a picture next to each one and explain why you have chosen that charge. For example, 'I've chosen holly because I always tell the truth.'

3 Design a coat of arms for your family. Choose the basic pattern, charges and colours. Remember not to break the basic colour rule. You may even like to create your own cardboard shield and paint your design on it.

Why do we give the 'V' sign as an insult?

AIMS

- What was the sequence of fighting in the Hundred Years' War?
- How can some modern customs have historical origins?

Most people know what the 'V' sign is. Sometimes people stick two fingers up to insult someone. If you haven't ever done it, I bet you know someone who has, or you've seen it on television. Believe it or not, English people have been sticking two fingers up as an insult for nearly 700 years.

It all started during the Hundred Years' War, a long series of battles between England and France that started in 1337. The English king, Edward III, enjoyed fighting and wanted the glory and excitement that went along with winning. His mother was a French princess, so he believed he had the right to be king of France. He was also unhappy that the French had been helping the Scots to fight England, and was keen to attack them to stop their aid to the Scots. Like most wars, the Hundred Years' War was a bit like a roller coaster, with its ups and downs. First one side did well, then the other side, and so on. Read the roller coaster story of the Hundred Years' War carefully and remember to look out for the 'V' sign insult along the way.

1340
"The English victory at sea at Sluys gives Edward control of the seas."

1346
"Edward's army of 12,000 men slaughter 24,000 French at Crécy. His archers shot 72,000 arrows in 90 seconds."

1347
"The English capture the port of Calais: why was this important?"

1356
"Edwar
leads 8,
against
king is c
ransom

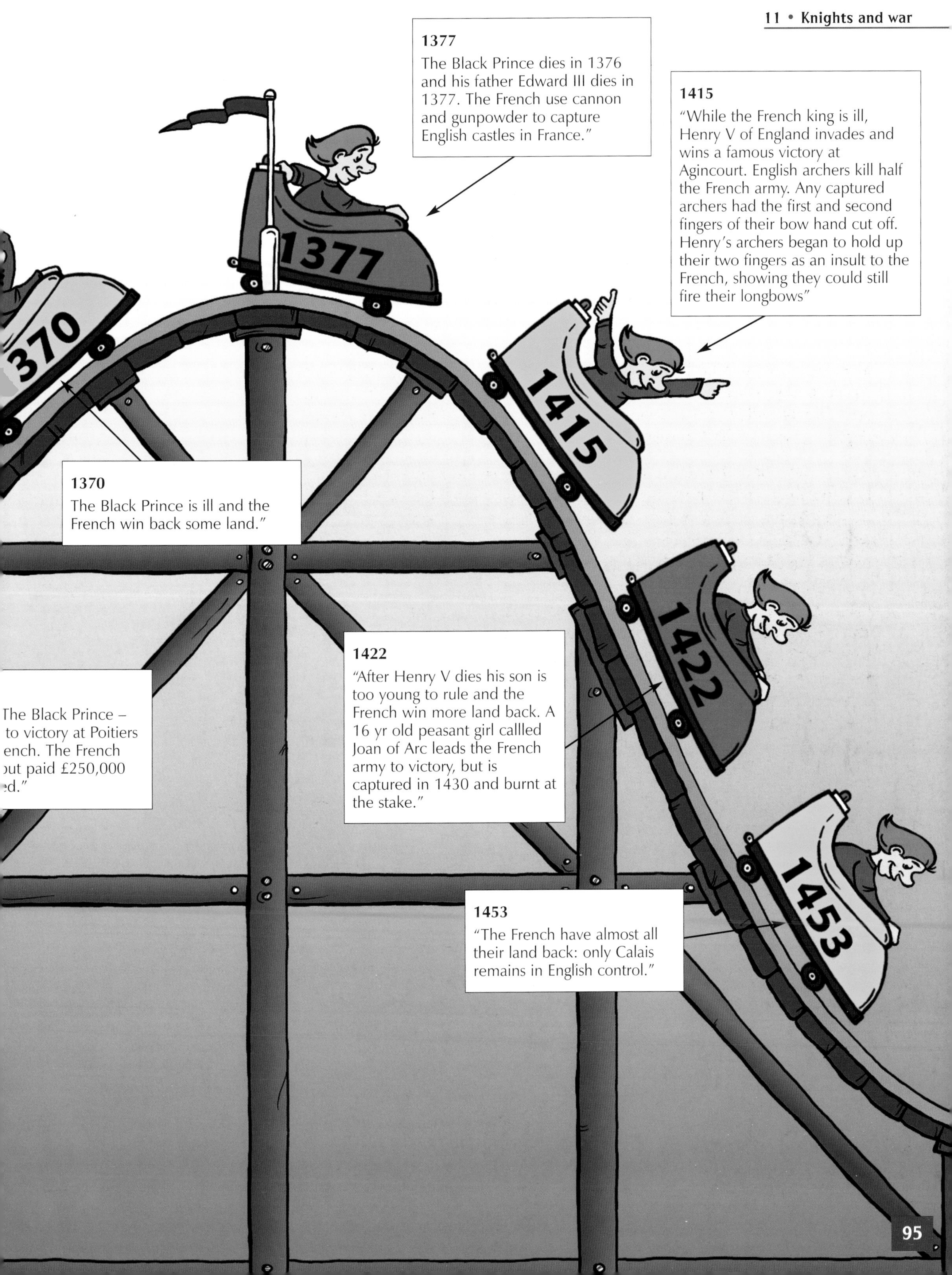
1377
The Black Prince dies in 1376 and his father Edward III dies in 1377. The French use cannon and gunpowder to capture English castles in France."
1415
"While the French king is ill, Henry V of England invades and wins a famous victory at Agincourt. English archers kill half the French army. Any captured archers had the first and second fingers of their bow hand cut off. Henry's archers began to hold up their two fingers as an insult to the French, showing they could still fire their longbows"
1377
370
1415
1370
The Black Prince is ill and the French win back some land."
1422
"After Henry V dies his son is too young to rule and the French win more land back. A 16 yr old peasant girl callled Joan of Arc leads the French army to victory, but is captured in 1430 and burnt at the stake."
1422
The Black Prince –
to victory at Poitiers
ench. The French
ut paid £250,000
d."
1453
"The French have almost all their land back: only Calais remains in English control."
1453

The Hundred Years' War didn't last for exactly 100 years – it lasted for 116 years. Despite famous English victories at Sluys, Crécy, Poitiers and Agincourt, the armies were never strong enough to defeat the French completely. After all, the French were defending their homeland so they must have put that extra bit of effort into saving their own country.

Source A ▸ an illustration from a French manuscript of the sea battle at Sluys

FACT: ▸ Blind courage

▸ King John of Bohemia was fighting for the French at the Battle of Crécy despite that fact that he was blind. He was so desperate to fight that he tied himself to two knights and charged into battle on his horse. He was hacked to pieces.

Source B ◂ this painting of the battle of Crécy is taken from a medieval French book

HUNGRY FOR MORE?

Joan of Arc was a fascinating character from the Hundred Years' War. She was a teenager who led an entire army, and she's still a national hero in France. Find out more about her and write a fact file on her, making sure you include details about her life and why she is still such a popular figure today.

FACT: The longbow

- The longbow was a deadly weapon. The bow was longer than the man who used it and was made from elm, yew or hazel wood. The string was made from hemp or linen. The wooden arrows were just under a metre long, with iron arrowheads and feather fletchings. A good archer could fire up to ten arrows a minute, killing a man up to 200 metres away.

Source A ▲ an illustration from a Dutch manuscript showing the Earl of Warwick in battle against the French. The English longbowmen are in the lower left of the picture

Now back to the question at the top of these pages. Why do we give the 'V' sign as an insult? The answer lies in the fact that the English archers or longbowmen were very good. If you look back at the roller coaster, it's the archers who always seemed to save the day.

If an archer was ever captured, the French would cut off the first two fingers on his right hand. Can you guess why? If an Englishman saw a captured Frenchman, he would run up to him and stick up his two fingers to show that he was still a threat. As the years went by this became an insult. If you didn't like someone, you would give them the 'V' sign with the first two fingers of your right hand!

WISE UP WORDS

charge chivalry dub heraldry homage joust mêlées page standard squire

WORK

1. The following dates were important in the Hundred Years' War. Write the dates in the correct chronological order. Then, in one sentence, write what happened in that year.

   1347 • 1430 • 1346 • 1370 • 1356 • 1377 • 1340 • 1422 • 1453 • 1376 • 1415

2. Make a list of turning points in the Hundred Years' War. Turning points are events that changed the course of the war. Explain why you chose them as turning points.

3. The French hated the English archers or longbowmen. Why do you think they were so feared?

Summary

- England was often at war with France in the Middle Ages.
- The Hundred Years' War between England and France actually lasted for 116 years.
- English longbowmen were important in defeating the French in battle.
- By 1453 the French had regained control of almost all the land previously lost to the English.

The Wars of the Roses

- When did the Wars of the Roses take place?
- What was the nature of power and power struggles in medieval England?

The Hundred Years' War ended in 1453 but England faced a serious problem. King Henry VI had gone mad! He had lost his memory, sitting quietly in the corner of his room for hours on end, finding it difficult to move without help. He didn't even know that his wife had given birth to a child, Prince Edward. His family – the Lancasters – didn't know what to do.

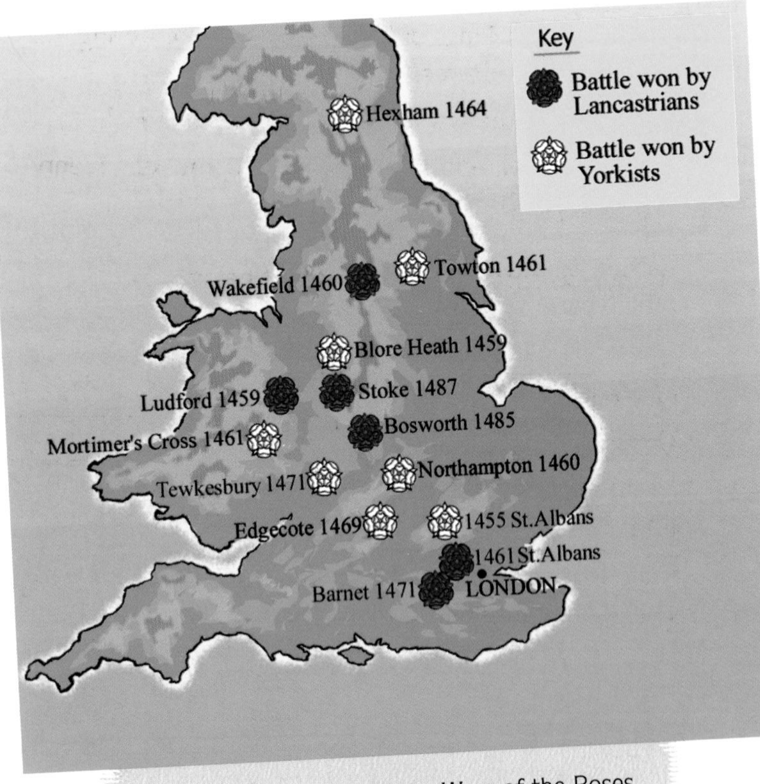

Source A ▲ Battles of the Wars of the Roses

Not surprisingly, a powerful rival family called the Yorks seized this opportunity to increase their power. Led by Edward York, they decided to fight King Henry and take over England. The two families, the Yorks and the Lancasters, chose different signs to put on their badges, banners and shields. The Lancasters chose a red rose; the Yorks chose a white rose. Over the next 30 years, the two sides would fight a series of wars that became known as the Wars of the Roses.

The two sides started fighting in 1455. First one side would win a battle and then the other. As a result, the country was not ruled very well throughout this period. Much of the fighting was done by soldiers who had fought in the Hundred Years' War and had now been hired by the different families. The battles were often very bloody, murderous affairs. After the Battle of Towton in 1461, local people said there was so much blood you could see red stains on the ground from miles away. Even today, the field where this battle took place is called the Bloody Meadow.

Source B ▼ Timeline of the Wars of the Roses

1399	1453	1461	1470	1471	1471 – 83	1483	1483-85	1485	22 August 1485
Lancaster family rule England.	Henry VI goes mad. Edward, Duke of York starts to fight for the crown.	Edward defeats Henry VI at the Battle of Towton. He becomes King Edward IV.	Henry VI defeats Edward IV. Henry takes the throne again.	Edward IV defeats Henry VI again. Henry VI is murdered.	Edward IV rules over England.	Edward IV dies. His young son, Prince Edward, should become king – but disappears. Edward IV's brother, Richard, takes over.	Richard III rules over England.	The last important member of the Lancaster family, Henry Tudor, challenges Richard III for the crown.	Battle of Boswor Field. Henry Tudor becomes Henry VII.

After 30 years of fighting, Henry Tudor defeated Richard III at the Battle of Bosworth Field in 1485. Henry Tudor became King Henry VII, the first Tudor king. Most people thought he would soon be killed by a supporter of the York family, but Henry held on to his throne and went on to rule England well. One reason why Henry was able to do this was because he cleverly married Elizabeth of York, a lady of importance in the house of York. This united the two families. He even joined the two roses together to make a new badge – the Tudor rose.

Source C ▸ Henry VI, who was murdered in May 1471

Source D ◂ Edward IV who was actually paid by France to return to England during his invasion

Summary

- Between 1399 and 1485 two families fought for the English crown
- The Lancaster family and the York family both had roses as family symbols, so the wars are known as the Wars of the Roses.
- Henry Tudor from the Lancaster family finally won the crown in 1485 after defeating King Richard III at Bosworth field.

WORK

1 Write these statements in the correct chronological order.
- First battle of the Wars of the Roses.
- Henry VI goes mad.
- The Battle of Bosworth Field takes place.
- The Hundred Years' War ends.
- Henry Tudor becomes king of England.

2 How did the Wars of the Roses get their name?

3 Study **Source B**.

a How long did the Wars of the Roses last?

b How many kings of England were there during the Wars of the Roses?

c Who was the last king of the House of York?

d In what year did Henry Tudor become King Henry VII of England?

4 Copy and complete the word grid below.

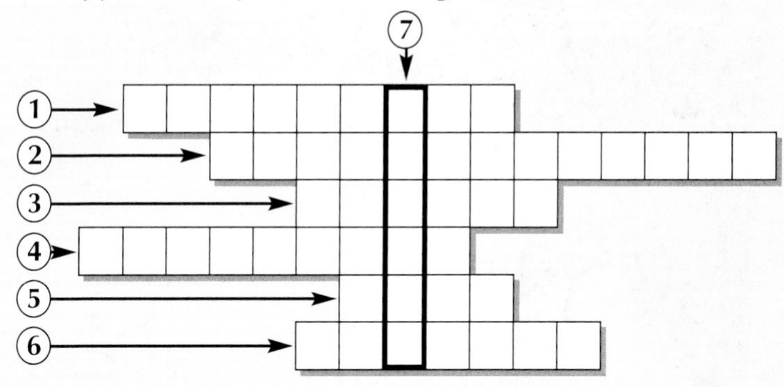

Clues

1 King Henry's family name.

2 The final battle of the Wars of the Roses.

3 Duke of York in 1453.

4 Married Henry Tudor, uniting the families of York and Lancaster.

5 King Richard III's family name.

6 Murdered in 1471.

Make up your own clue for downword 7.

HISTORY MYSTERY

The princes in the tower

This is one of history's greatest mysteries. This fascinating 'whodunnit' has had historians baffled for over 500 years. When you have looked at the evidence, see if you can draw any conclusions.

Edward IV loved drinking, dancing and hunting. Most of all he loved eating. After one huge meal in April 1483, he was so full that he went to bed for hours. He caught a fever there and died. His son, also called Edward, travelled to London to be crowned. His other son, Richard, was due to join them later. Prince Edward was 12 years old and Prince Richard was 10.

The two boys stayed in the Tower of London while Prince Edward prepared for his **coronation**. The boys' uncle, also called Richard, had been asked to look after the princes and help young Edward until he could rule the country on his own.

In June a rumour started to spread across London. People were saying that young Prince Edward's father had not been married to his mother. This meant that Prince Edward couldn't become King. The Bishop of Bath said that the rumours were true, so two weeks later Prince Edward's uncle, Richard, was crowned king instead. He became King Richard III.

But what about the two boys? In the summer of 1483, they were seen playing in the gardens of the Tower of London. After that, they were never seen again. What had happened to them? Could they have been murdered? If so, who did it? The history mystery detectives need to investigate!

Evidence A

Written in 1483

Prince Edward and his brother were taken to the inner rooms of the tower, and day by day began to be seen less behind the bars and the windows, until they stopped appearing altogether.

Evidence B

A speech by a Frenchman in 1484

Look at what has happened since the death of King Edward. His courageous children have been killed and the crown has gone to their murderer.

Evidence E

In 1674 some workmen were working on a staircase in the Tower of London. Two metres underground they discovered a box full of bones. The bones were reburied in Westminster Abbey. They are still there today.

Evidence C

Written in the Great Chronicle of London, 1512

The children were seen shooting and playing in the garden until Easter [1484]. After Easter there was much whispering among the people that the king had put the children to death.

Evidence G

In 1955 other doctors looked at the report made in 1933. They weren't allowed to look at the bones but studied pictures instead. They said that:

- *the bones were from children younger than the two princes*
- *the stain was not caused by suffocation.*

Evidence D

Written in 1513 by Sir Thomas More. More was brought up by John Morton, a man who hated Richard III because he put him in prison in 1483.

King Richard wanted Sir James Tyrell to carry out his wishes. Tyrell decided that the princes should be murdered in their beds. He picked Miles Forest and John Dighton to do the job.

About midnight Forest and Dighton entered the room where the children lay in their beds and forced the feather bed and pillows hard into their mouths until they stopped breathing.

They laid their bodies out naked on the bed and fetched Sir James to see them. Then he got the murderers to bury them at the bottom of the stairs, deep in the ground under a heap of stones. Later a priest dug up the bodies and moved them to a place which only he knew.

Evidence H

By historian Phillip Lindsay in 1972

Richard had no reason to kill them. Henry Tudor had every reason. Henry was capable of such a crime, so they were quietly murdered.

Evidence I

There were many rumours at the time. Some said that the two boys had fallen off a bridge. Others said that Prince Edward had become ill and died naturally and Prince Richard was secretly taken abroad.

Evidence J

When Henry Tudor became king he gave land and important jobs to James Tyrell, John Dighton and Miles Forest

Evidence F

In 1933 two doctors examined the bones. Their report said:

- *the skeletons were not complete*
- *the bones belonged to two children aged about 10 and 12*
- *a stain on one of the skulls may mean that they could have been suffocated*
- *the bones could have been there since 1100*
- *the elder boy had a serious tooth disease.*

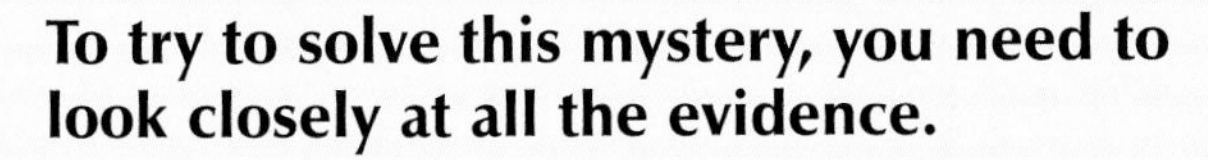

WORK

To try to solve this mystery, you need to look closely at all the evidence.

1 **Find out about the events leading up to the disappearance of the two princes.**

Think about where and when the princes were last seen. Why were they there?

2 **Find a motive – who might want them dead and why?**

Is there anybody who might benefit from the princes' deaths? Why are Richard III and Henry Tudor both suspects? Explain your ideas.

3 **Find any evidence to show it might not have been a murder.**

Perhaps the boys died of natural causes?Write down any ideas you have to support this theory.

4 **Find any evidence for murder.**

Is there any evidence to support the idea that the two princes were murdered? If so, how and by whom?

5 **Consider whose evidence might not be reliable.**

Could someone be making things up? Why might someone lie? Does any one piece of evidence **contradict** another? Write down your theories.

6 **Now make your decision.**

Write a short paragraph to explain what you think happened to the princes in the tower.

Have you been learning?

Note: you might find answers to some questions are in pages 104–109

Task 1

Find the following words in the wordsearch below. They can be found across, down, up and diagonally. Each time you find a word, write a sentence about it.

archery • wrestling • hunting • stoolball • bowling • tennis • draughts • golf • conkers • chess • football • coldhand

G	N	I	L	W	O	B	A	Y
B	S	H	U	N	T	I	N	G
L	T	S	I	N	N	E	T	N
C	O	N	K	E	R	S	F	I
F	O	O	T	B	A	L	L	L
E	L	L	A	R	O	G	C	T
M	B	N	D	G	E	H	G	S
K	A	R	C	H	E	R	Y	E
T	L	G	I	S	A	E	W	R
V	L	E	S	R	O	N	D	W
S	T	H	G	U	A	R	D	F

Task 3

Here is a list of ways in which characters in this book died. Match the grim deaths to the unlucky person. They are not all kings and you may find two people who died the same way.

a Arrow through the throat in battle.

b Suffocated with his brother.

c Beheaded in the middle of the lord's prayer.

d Bladder burst in a riding accident.

e Ate too many peaches.

f Leprosy.

g An arrow in the eye.

h Red-hot poker up the bottom.

i Fell into a toilet.

j Burned at the stake.

Task 3

Complete the following names from the Middle Ages. Look at the clues and fill in the missing consonants.

a) _ i _ _ a _ _   _ _ e   _ i o _ _ e a _ _
(three lions)

b) _ e o _ _ _ e _   _ _ a u _ e _
(Canterbury Tales)

c) _ i _ _ i a _   _ a _ _ a _ e
(Braveheart)

d) _ i _ _ i a _   _ _ e   _ o _ _ u e _ o _
(winner in 1066)

e) _ o _ e _ _   _ _ u _ e
(winner at Bannockburn)

f) _ _ o _ a _   _ e _ _ e _
(friend then enemy of Henry II)

g) _ a _ a _ _   _ a _ _ _ a _ a
(sore throat in 1066)

h) _ i _ _ i a _   _ u _ u _
(Red Billy)

i) _ _ _ _ e _ _ _   a _ _   _ a _ _ _ _
(Welsh brothers)

j) _ o a _   o _   A _ _
(16 years old)

k) _ a _   _ _ _ e _
(peasant leader)

l) _ i _ o _   _ e   _ o _ _ _ o _ _
(no friend of Henry III)

m) _ i _ _ i a _   _ a _ _ o _
(printer)

n) _ a _ a _ i _
(Saracen leader)

o) _ e _ _ _   _ u _ o _
(winner in 1485)

Task 4

The sentences below don't make much sense. They need capital letters, commas, full stops and apostrophes.

a Copy the sentences, adding punctuation as you write.

- the battles of stamford bridge and hastings were both in 1066
- william the conqueror was king of england for 21 years
- the best weapons to attack a castle were the siege tower the trebuchet and the battering ram
- king henry always felt guilty about thomas beckets murder in canterbury cathedral
- richard the lionhearts finest victory was at the battle of acre in 1191
- king edwards nickname was the hammer of the scots
- the black death was first reported in china and india in 1334
- richard II was englands finest king
- at the battle of agincourt in 1415 king henrys army defeated the French army easily
- henry tudor became king after he defeated king richard in the battle of bosworth field

b In each sentence, underline the facts in blue and the opinions in red.

Task 5

This picture shows archers practising their shooting in 1340. Archers were a very important part of the English army. Some kings even banned football because men were spending too much time playing and not enough time practising their archery skills.

Write a weapon fact file on the longbow. Include the following details.

Facts

- What was the longbow made from?
- How long was it?
- What about the arrows – how far could they go?
- How many arrows could be fired in a minute?

Impact

- In which battles was the longbow used?
- In which wars was the longbow used?
- Did the longbow change the outcome of the battles?

Task 6

a Here are six groups of words or names. In each group there is an odd one out. When you think you have found it, write a sentence or two to explain why you think it doesn't fit in with any of the others.

1. Agincourt • Poitiers • Jaffa • Crécy
2. archery • golf • bowling • baseball
3. fire • murder • combat • water
4. gold • red • purple • blue
5. Henry I • Richard II • King John • Edward IV
6. theft • stocks • pillory • scold's bridle

b Now make up your own 'odd one out' word sets. Make three sets and then try them out on a classmate. Can they find the odd one out?

Medieval England: How did England change?

AIMS
- What changes took place in England between 1066 and 1485?
- How did new inventions change things?

This book covers the period from 1066 to 1485. We started and ended our story with two important battles. In 1066 William the Conqueror beat King Harold at Hastings. In 1485 Henry Tudor beat Richard III at Bosworth Field. The time just before 1066 is known as the Anglo-Saxon period. The time after 1485 is known as the Tudor period. The time in between is known as the Middle Ages.

Historians like to give labels to different periods of time. Nobody used the phrase 'the Middle Ages' at the time – the label was invented much later. But, no matter what we call the years between 1066 and 1485, we know that a lot of changes took place. These pages try to highlight the most important ones.

Why do you think the population went up and then back down?

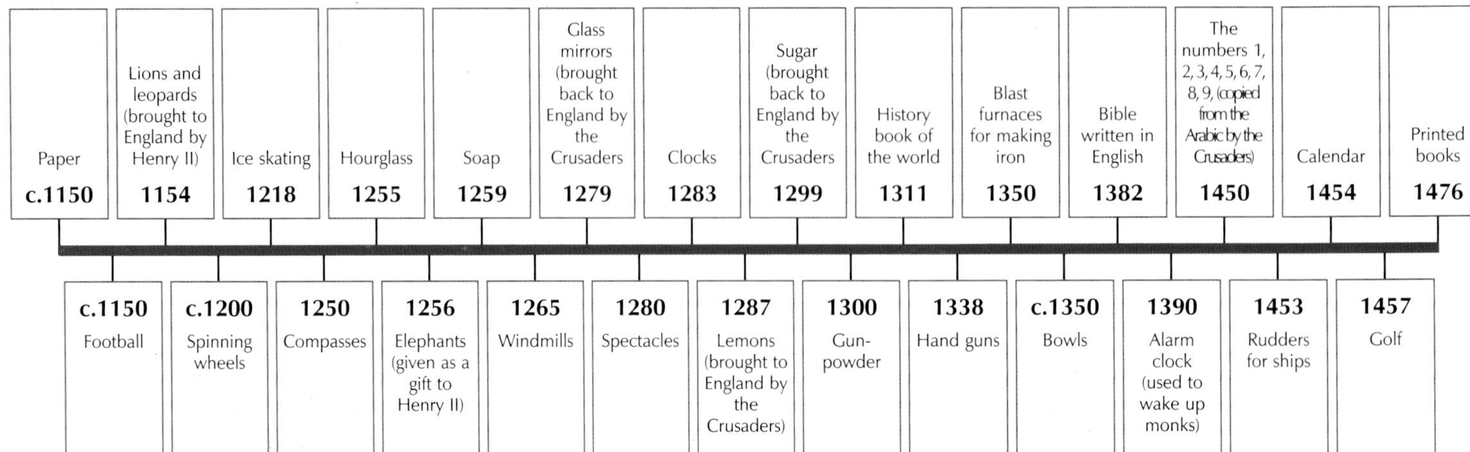

The big bang

Gunpowder changed battles and wars for ever. It was used to fire cannons and handguns. Swords, axes, and bows and arrows were no match for a man with a handgun or cannon. Even castle walls could be knocked down easily. In 1464 Bamburgh Castle in Northumberland was the first castle to have its walls knocked down by a cannon. Soon, lords began to build castles for comfort rather than defence. They would still include a strongroom or tower in case of attack, but castles were smaller, made from brick, with much thinner walls, more doors and larger windows.

WORK

1 Inventions change things. For example, the invention of the passenger aeroplane meant that we could travel further and faster than ever before. Think about the following inventions:

- the spinning wheel, for winding wool into threads
- gunpowder
- compasses and rudders for ships
- printed books.

Write a few sentences about each discovery, saying why each of them was important and how you think it might have helped to change things.

2 Look back at pages 6 and 7, which give details about England before the Norman invasion. Using the information on these pages, and what you have read about in the rest of this book, answer the following question.

How was the England of 1485 different to the England of 1065?

Chose an invention or discovery from the timeline. Research it carefully. Who invented it? When? Where? How? Was there a special reason for its invention or discovery? How has it developed? It is still used today? If so, where? You could work in small groups and present your findings to the rest of your class.

Was it dangerous to be king?

- What medieval monarchs ruled from 1066 to 1485?
- How did each medieval monarch die?

In 1066 King Harold of England was killed at the Battle of Hastings. An arrow hit him, possibly in his eye, and after he fell to the floor a group of William's knights hacked him to pieces with their swords. In 1485 Richard III was dragged from his horse while fighting at the Battle of Bosworth Field against Henry Tudor. Some of Henry's soldiers cut him to bits, possibly found his bloodstained crown in a thorn bush and placed it on Henry Tudor's head. He became Henry VII, the first Tudor king.

The Middle Ages start in about 1066 and end in 1485. You have covered these dates in this book. The death of these two kings makes it sound like being king of England was a dangerous job... but was it?

King Harold of England (1066)
Killed at the Battle of Hastings in 1066

◆ William I (1066–87)
Killed when his bladder burst in a riding accident. Died in agony.

◆ William II (Rufus) (1087–1100)
Shot and killed in a hunting accident. (But was it an accident?)

◆ Henry I (1100–35)
Spent a lot of time fighting with his brothers. Died of eating too much.

◆ Stephen (1135–54)
Spent most of his time fighting for the throne against his cousin Matilda (who did rule briefly in 1141). Died of dysentery and infected piles.

◆ Henry II (1154–89)
His wife and two sons spent years trying to kill him. Died while fighting a war against them.

◆ Richard I (The Lionheart) (1189–99)
Shot in the neck by an arrow while fighting in France. The wound became infected when doctors tried to dig out the arrow tip. Died as a result of the infection.

◆ John (Lackland) (1199–1216)
Spent a lot of his time arguing with his barons. Died from dysentery, made worse by eating too many peaches.

◆ Henry III (1216–72)
Thrown into prison by Simon de Montfort in 1264. Eventually regained his throne in 1265 but had lost the respect of his barons. Died of old age.

◆ Edward I (Hammer of the Scots) (1272–1307)
Died of dysentery while on his way to fight the Scots.

◆ Edward II (1307–27)
Lost all the land in Scotland that his father had won. Hated by his wife Isabella, who wanted their son to be king instead. She tried to poison him by throwing him in a prison cell over a rubbish pit. She eventually killed him by ordering two men to stick a red-hot iron up his bottom!

◆ Edward III (1327–77)
Ruled during the Black Death. Died aged 64 of a stroke.

◆ **Richard II (1377–99)**
Had no children. Was put in prison by his cousin Henry IV, who then took over the throne. He was eventually starved to death in Pontefract Castle.

▼

◆ **Henry IV (1399–1413)**
Some say that he had so many lice in his hair that it wouldn't grow. He caught leprosy and died a badly disfigured man.

▼

◆ **Henry V (1413–22)**
Died of dysentery while fighting in France.

▼

◆ **Henry VI (1422–61 and 1470–71)**
Fought the Wars of the Roses. Went mad, lost his throne twice and was murdered in the Tower of London.

▼

◆ **Edward IV (1461–70 and 1471–83)**
Fought the Wars of the Roses. Caught a fever and died after eating too much.

▼

◆ **Edward V (1483–?)**
Disappeared aged 12, possibly suffocated.

▼

◆ **Richard III (1483–85)**
Killed at the Battle of Bosworth Field.

▼

◆ **Henry VII (1485–1509)**
Ended the Wars of the Roses by marrying Elizabeth of York, a member of the opposing family. Died of pneumonia.

Key

- ◆ Norman, because they first lived in Normandy, France
- ◆ Plantagent – family name
- ◆ Lancaster – family name
- ◆ York – family name
- ◆ Tudor – family name

FACT: The name game

- Historians give names to the different groups or families who ruled England between 1066 and 1485. This also makes it easier to remember the stories about them.

WORK

1. Make notes of how many kings were killed by the following:
   battle • accident • eating too much • murder • old age • illness
2. Draw a bar chart to show your findings.
3. What was the biggest cause of death? Why do you think this was so high?
4. Which cause of death surprises you the most? Explain your answer.
5. Write a paragraph to answer the following question: 'Was being a medieval king of England a dangerous job?'

HUNGRY FOR MORE?

The diagram looks at 20 kings and one queen (remember Matilda). Five of the rulers were under 15 years of age when they became king. But who were they? Try to find out the names and ages of the five youngest kings – one was only eight months old. He sat on his mother's knee and cried when he was crowned! Another king's head was so small that they had to use a bracelet as a crown!

Who saved the English Language?

- How can we see the influence of history in modern life?
- What are the origins of the language we speak?

What is the official language of England? English, of course. But did you know that for many years after the Norman Conquest it was the third most important language in England. So how did it regain its number one spot?

Before 1066 the people of England spoke a language called **Old English**. This was a mixture of different languages taken from the various peoples who had invaded England over the years.

Source A ▾ An Old English song

Summer is coming in, loud now sing cuckoo,
Seeds grow, breezes blow and trees shout out anew
The ewe bleats for her lamb,
The cow lows for her calf,
The bullock starts
The buck farts,
Merrily sing cuckoo.

In 1066 William the Conqueror brought the French language to England. King Harold, the man he had killed at Hastings, was the last English-speaking king for 300 years. All the important men William brought over from France spoke French – the king himself, the queen, the barons, their wives and their children.

They brought new words with them – words that we still know today like battle, baron, enemy, castle, army, arrest, archer, judge, traitor, prison, guard, market, city, sausage, grape, sugar and plate. They could also speak Latin, a living language in 1066, taught in schools and cathedrals and spoken by educated people all over Europe.

Old English was by now officially the third most important language in England.

Two hundred years after the Norman Conquest, written English was dead. Nobody wrote it any more and nobody seemed to care. Kings and nobles spoke French; churchmen, teachers and **merchants** spoke Latin. Books handwritten by monks were written in Latin too. The only people who seemed to speak English were the peasants, but how they spoke varied from place to place in England. Peasants couldn't read or write either. William the Conqueror, William II, Henry I, Stephen, Henry II, Richard I, John, Henry III, Edward I and Edward II all spoke French as their first language. The disappearing English language needed a saviour!

Do some of the new French words have anything in common? Clue: Were the English and the French the best of friends at the time?

Contestant 1: Geoffrey Chaucer

- A poet from London who spoke French, Latin and English.
- Wrote The Canterbury Tales, a collection of stories about a group of pilgrims on their way to see Thomas Becket's tomb.
- Wrote in English, the language of ordinary people, but used French words when he didn't think an English one fitted. For example, instead of using the word 'hard' (English) he would choose the word 'difficult' (French) instead. He thought English was a brilliant language to write in because he had so many words to choose from – words that came from Old English, French, Latin, Norse and Anglo-Saxon.
- Reintroduced some words that hadn't been written down since 1100, such as friendly, learning, wasp, farting, learning.

Contestant 2: King Edward III

- Realised that English was still spoken by many ordinary people.
- Was the first king to allow English to be spoken in parliament.
- Allowed court cases to be held in English in 1362.

Contestant 3: King Henry IV

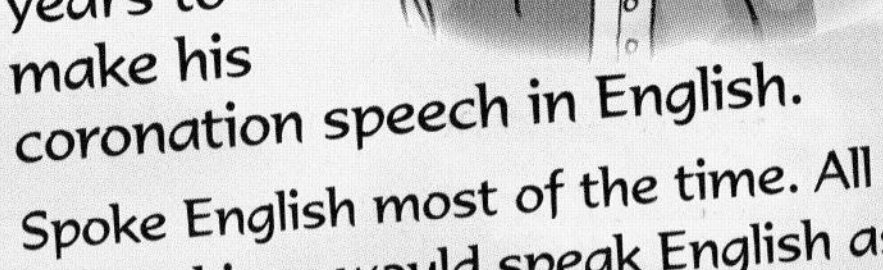

- In 1399 became the first king in over 300 years to make his coronation speech in English.
- Spoke English most of the time. All future kings would speak English as their first language. Remember, if the king spoke the language, so did all the rich and powerful people.

Contestant 4: William Caxton

- Was the first English printer. Began printing books in 1476.
- Printed copies of nearly 100 books, including The Canterbury Tales in 1483.
- English replaced Latin as the language of books. More ordinary people began to read books because now they could understand them. By 1500 about 30 out of 100 people could read.
- More books became available than ever before. The ideas in them could be read and discussed all over the country.

WISE UP WORDS

merchants old English norse

WORK

1. In pairs or small groups, discuss who did the most to save the English language. Was it Edward III, Henry IV, Geoffrey Chaucer or William Caxton?
2. Decide who you think did the most to save the English language. Write a paragraph explaining why you think this person's actions were the most important.
3. Take on the role of your chosen character. See if you can convince the rest of your class that your character had the biggest effect on saving the English language. The class should then vote on who has presented the strongest case.

Glossary

Abbey A large monastery.

Abbot The head monk in an abbey.

Anglo-Saxons Invaders from Germany who ruled from about 500 to 1066.

Apothecaries People who made and sold medicines made from herbs and plants.

Archbishop An important church leader. The Archbishop of Canterbury was in charge of all the churches in England.

Bailey A large courtyard surrounded by a fence, part of a castle.

Barber-surgeon A medieval equivalent of a doctor.

Baron An important person who looked after an area of land for the king.

Besiege To surround a castle or town and try to capture it.

Blood-letting The practice of making someone bleed to help cure an illness.

Cavalry Soldiers on horses.

Chancellor An important job helping the king.

Charter A written agreement or set of promises.

Chivalry A special code of behaviour for knights.

Christian A person who believes in God and follows the teachings of his son, Jesus Christ.

Chronicles Diary of events.

Chronological order The order in which events happened, starting with the earliest.

Church This can mean one building or an entire Christian community, such as the Roman Catholic Church.

Commons Representatives of ordinary people in Parliament.

Contradict Argue against.

Coronation The crowning of a king or queen.

Crenels The gaps on top of castle towers or walls.

Crusades Holy wars in which Crusaders from Europe set out to fight Muslim Turks.

Daub Mud, dung and straw, smeared over wattle to make a wall.

Disembowelled To cut open someone's stomach and pull out their insides, used as a punishment.

Dowry Money or gifts given to a husband by his wife's family after marriage.

Dub To touch a man on the shoulder with a sword as he becomes a knight.

Dysentery A disease which causes terrible diarrhoea.

Earldom An area of land that an earl looks after.

Earls Important men who look after an area of land for the king.

Evidence Information that helps a person to form an opinion.

Excommunicated This is when someone is banned from going to church – a terrible punishment in the Middle Ages as it meant you would go to hell when you died.

Fallow Land left alone, to allow it to get its goodness back.

Feudal system A system of dividing up land; men received land in return for offering to fight or provide a service for their lord.

Flagellants People who whipped themselves in order to ask God to forgive them for their sins.

Franks The word used by Saracens to describe the Crusaders.

Freeman A person who is free from his duties to his lord.

Fyrd King Harold's ordinary soldiers.

Guild A club or society of traders and merchants.

Heir Next in line to be king or queen.

Heraldry The study of coats of arms.

Hermit A man who lives on his own and has no contact with anybody.

Homage A promise of loyalty to the king.

Housecarls One of King Harold's best soldiers.

Hue and cry A noisy group of people who chased criminals.

Inferior Of poor quality.

Infirmary Medieval version of a hospital, often attached to a monastery.

Inherit To receive a person's land and/or belongings after his death.

Jester An entertainer who toured castles and towns telling silly stories and singing.

Joust A sport in which two knights on horses fought each other.

Jury A group of people who decide if a person is guilty or innocent of a crime.

Keep The strongest part of a castle.

Knights Men who promise to fight for their lord.

Lance A weapon; a long spear usually tipped with steel.

Latin An Ancient Roman language, still popular in the Middle Ages.

Leeches Blood-sucking creatures used in medieval medicine.

Looting Stealing.

Lord A person above another in the feudal system.

Loyalty Faithfulness; if a person promised loyalty, they promised to support someone.

Mêlées Huge fights between large teams of knights.

Medieval Another word for Middle Ages.

Merchants People who buy and sell things.

Monarch A king or queen.

Monastery A building where monks live.

Monks Men who dedicate their life to worshipping God.

Motive The reason for doing something.

Motte A large mound of earth on which a keep is usually built.

Muslims People who believe in a God called Allah, and that a prophet called Muhammad was a messenger from Allah.

Nobles Rich and powerful men like barons or earls.

Norman A man from Normandy, an area of France.

Norse Viking language.

Novice A boy training to be a monk.

Nun A woman who dedicates her life to worshipping God.

Nunnery A building where nuns live.

Old English A mixture of languages used in England before 1066.

Ordeal A medieval way of finding out if a person was guilty of a crime or not.

Page A young boy training to be a knight.

Pardons Special letters that forgive a person for a crime.

Parliament The body of Lords and Commons set up to rule the country with the King.

Peasants Ordinary poor farmers who do not own much land, if any at all.

Pilgrim A person who makes a journey to a holy place.

Pilgrimage A religious journey.

Pillory A wooden frame with holes for head and hands, used as a punishment.

Plague A disease, usually used to describe the Black Death.

Poll tax A tax that everyone pays; people all paid the same amount no matter what they could afford.

Pope The leader of the Roman Catholic Church.

Prophet Someone sent by God to tell His message.

Ransom Money paid for captured knights to let them go free.

Rebel Someone who takes part in a rebellion or uprising.

Rebellion A group of people who fight or protest.

Revolt Another word for a rebellion or uprising.

Sanctuary A safe place, such as a church.

Sappers Soldiers who would dig under a castle wall.

Saracens The word used by the Crusaders to describe Muslims.

Scold's bridle A head brace used to punish a nagging wife, sometimes called a Scold's brace.

Scriptorium A writing room in a monastery.

Siege A situation where a group of soldiers try to capture a town or castle; the defenders try to stop the attackers from getting in.

Sheriffs Men who helped keep law and order.

Shield wall A long line of shields in a battle.

Squire A teenager training to be a knight.

Standard A flag or emblem of a knight or Baron.

Stocks A wooden frame with holes for feet, used as a punishment.

Symptoms Signs of illness or disease.

Tithe A tax that people had to pay to the local priest, usually one tenth of their farm produce.

Tonsure A monk's bald patch on the top of his head.

Tournament A collection of games, hunts and mock battles for knights.

Traitor Someone who betrays the king.

Treason A crime against the king or queen.

Trepanning Drilling a hole in a patient's head in the belief that this would cure their headache.

Truce A temporary break in a battle or war.

Tunic A covering robe, usually worn over chain mail.

Turbulent Troublesome.

Turks A tribe of Muslim warriors who moved to the Holy Land.

Uprising A rebellion.

Vellum Parchment made from calf skin used for writing on.

Vikings Invader from Denmark, Sweden or Norway.

Villeins Peasants.

Wattle Sticks woven together.

Witan Before the Normans arrived in England, this was a group of the most important bishops and earls.

Index